D1761444

EAT

Branding & Design
for Takeaways
& Restaurants

Wang Shaoqiang (ed.)

GO

promopress

EAT & GO

Branding & Design for Takeaways & Restaurants
Design de marques pour la restauration rapide
Diseño de marca para takeaways y restaurantes
Design de marca para takeaway e restaurantes

Editor: Wang Shaoqiang
English preface revised by: Tom Corkett
Translators of the preface:
Marie-Pierre Teuler French translation
Jesús de Cos Pinto Spanish translation
Élcio Carillo Portuguese (Brazilian) translation

Copyright © 2014 by Sandu Publishing Co., Ltd.
Copyright © 2014 English language edition by
Promopress for sale in Europe and America.
Reprinted 2017

PROMOPRESS is a brand of:
Promotora de Prensa Internacional S.A.
C/ Ausiàs March, 124
08013 Barcelona, Spain
Phone: 0034 93 245 14 64
Fax: 0034 93 265 48 83
info@promopress.es
www.promopresseditions.com
Facebook: Promopress Editions
Twitter: Promopress Editions @PromopressEd

Sponsored by Design 360°
– Concept and Design Magazine
Edited and produced by
Sandu Publishing Co., Ltd.
Book design, concepts & art direction by
Sandu Publishing Co., Ltd.
info@sandupublishing.com

cover design: spread: David Lorente with the
collaboration of Claudia Parra

ISBN 978-84-16504-91-6

Printed in Bosnia and Herzegovina

CONTENTS

DANIL SNITKO

ART DIRECTOR AT PUNK YOU BRANDS BRANDING AGENCY
WWW.PUNK-YOU.RU

You get out of bed in the morning with your eyes barely open. You'd hit snooze on your alarm clock whilst you were half asleep and now you're hastily hopping on one leg through your apartment, pulling on your clothes and getting your work stuff together at the same time. Breakfast is out of the question. You can no longer remember when you last had time to actually sip a cup of coffee before work in the morning. "Maybe I can stop in at a coffee shop and pick up a coffee and something to eat," you say to yourself. It's more or less the same idea as the one that flashes through the minds of millions of city dwellers every day.

Restaurants and other food outlets that offer takeaway services are actively gaining customers. This is especially evident in major metropolitan areas, where every second commuter is in a hurry to get somewhere. We no longer have time for leisurely walks, long lunches or sitting down for a cup of coffee.

Increased competition and a different kind of communication with the customer require a completely different approach to branding in this area. Brand-design options are no longer limited to creating signs and menus. They must attract the consumer in the midst of all the turmoil that constantly prevails in the life of a person living in a busy city.

The packaging design of takeaway products is also very important. Branding of takeaway restaurants is different from that of classic sit-in restaurants, and revolves round a distinct set of issues. To get the customer's attention it needs to be extraordinary, but it should not be too eccentric, since often the customer will eat their food directly out of this packaging.

Humans are emotional creatures. Every day we look for new feelings and experiences, even though this need is not as prominent as the sensation of hunger. It is not surprising that brands with a deeply emotional design are becoming very popular. Buying food or drink to take away is a spontaneous process, and decision making in this situation is governed by the customer's emotions.

We also need to keep in mind the fact that hunting for food is one of the basic survival instincts. Any information related to food is analysed in a part of our brain that was programmed millions of years ago. Before we have managed to consciously decide if we want this snack or not our brain already knows it's not going to happen because it smells bad or looks wrong. Exactly how wrong? "I don't know, but trust me: it's not worth it!" this ancient part of our brain tells us, and we listen to it because ignoring it may cost us dear. And you have to admit, after millions of years our brain is still pretty good at knowing how to define food that's fit to eat.

And so design that has anything to do with food, whether it is in the form of packaging or restaurant branding, faces some delicate challenges. It too is being analysed by the primitive part of our brain in order to decide whether it edible or not. That is why in this area, as in many others, the designer or agency always bears great responsibility for the result. Any wrong move, any error in reasoning can lead to a commercial failure. For example, in one case changing the label on a make of bread from red to green literally killed a brand. It turned out that the colour green on a loaf of bread is perceived as mould, which triggered people's brains and instincts to tell them that this bread was best avoided. Before even checking the expiration date the design led to the bread being rejected within a millisecond.

Whilst working on branding for a takeaway outlet the design team has to investigate not only the market and competitive environment but also, and even more importantly, how the brain analyses information about food. Which colour combinations seem enjoyable and "edible" and which do not? Which material suggests the product is organic and natural, and why? How will the customer interact with the product? Which forms and images are appropriate, and which will trigger the panic mode of the customer's brain and instincts?

In addition to the universal principles of design evaluation, it is essential to take into account the local cultural context. A design or product name that is clearly perceived as pleasant and appealing in one place can cause exactly the opposite reaction somewhere else. Whenever a design is developed or adapted for a new region it is necessary to carry out a study of the local cultural context.

Finally, functionality is extremely important when it comes to takeaways. A business might have packaging for a product—but is it suitable for carrying that product? Will the coffee spill when you open the lid if it is on too tight? Will the contents of a packet scatter everywhere because the packaging is made from a material that is too dense, meaning the consumer is forced to apply too much force in trying to open it? And if you put the product on a table, will it stand up? Will the cardboard get wet and soggy during prolonged storage or from condensation when heated in the microwave? Finally, can it be disposed of in an appropriate way?

Thousands of designers and agencies worldwide are working on all of these questions—and hundreds of others—on a daily basis. This book takes you into their world, revealing the conundrums faced by designers and the creative solutions they've come up with when working in this fascinating field.

And now, having had to skip breakfast this morning, I think it's time for me to go and grab a coffee and a bite to eat…

DANIL SNITKO

DIRECTEUR ARTISTIQUE CHEZ PUNK YOU BRANDS, AGENCE DE BRANDING
WWW.PUNK-YOU.RU

Ce matin, vous vous levez les yeux encore remplis de sommeil. Vous aviez repoussé la sonnerie du réveil et vous voilà en retard, parcourant l'appartement à cloche-pied pour tenter de vous habiller tout en préparant vos affaires de bureau. Pas question de prendre un petit-déjeuner. Vous ne vous rappelez même plus de la dernière fois où vous avez eu le temps de siroter un café avant d'aller travailler. Vous comptez vous arrêter dans un café pour commander la formule avec croissant que vous engloutirez en arrivant au bureau. Vous n'êtes pas le seul. Tous les matins, des millions de citadins font comme vous.

Les restaurants et autres établissements qui proposent de la nourriture à emporter attirent de plus en plus de clients. Cela est encore plus vrai dans les grandes villes où les banlieusards se bousculent pressés d'arriver quelque part. De nos jours, plus personne n'a le temps de se promener tranquillement, de déjeuner à loisir ou de s'assoire pour prendre un café.

Dans ce secteur la concurrence est féroce, et le rapport avec le client est différent. C'est pourquoi il faut complètement repenser la notion de marque. Le branding ne doit pas se limiter à la création d'enseignes et de menus. Son objectif est d'attirer le client étourdi par l'agitation permanente des grandes villes.

Le packaging des produits à emporter revêt également une importance capitale. La déclinaison d'une marque d'un établissement de vente à emporter est complètement différente de celle d'un restaurant classique. Son branding est axé sur des points très spécifiques. La marque devra être suffisamment originale pour attirer l'attention, mais sans tomber dans l'extravagance, parce que le plus souvent le client consommera directement les produits dans l'emballage fourni.

Nous sommes des êtres émotionnels. Nous cherchons en permanence à vivre de nouvelles émotions et expériences, même si ce besoin n'est pas aussi impérieux que la sensation de faim. Il n'est pas étonnant, dès lors, que les marques basées sur un concept émotionnel deviennent si populaires. L'achat de boisson ou de nourriture à emporter est un acte spontané, et la prise de décision du consommateur est gouvernée par ses émotions.

N'oublions pas que la recherche de nourriture fait partie de nos instincts de survie élémentaires. Toute information liée aux aliments est analysée par une partie de notre cerveau programmée il y a des millions d'années. Avant de décider au niveau conscient si nous voulons ou non le produit proposé, notre cerveau le rejette déjà parce qu'il ne sent pas bon ou qu'il n'a pas un bel aspect. Qu'est-ce qui ne va pas exactement ? « Je ne sais pas, mais fais-moi confiance : dis non ! », nous souffle notre cerveau reptilien, et nous l'écoutons parce qu'ignorer ses conseils pourrait nous coûter très cher. Force est de constater qu'après des millions d'années, notre cerveau sait toujours ce qui est bon à manger.

Ainsi, tout concept qui a trait à la nourriture, que ce soit pour un emballage ou une marque de restaurant, n'est pas si simple. Il sera analysé par notre cerveau ancestral qui jugera si le produit est mangeable ou pas. À cet égard, le créateur du concept ou l'agence est en grande partie responsable du résultat, toute mauvaise décision ou erreur de jugement pouvant se traduire par un échec commercial retentissant. Par exemple, le fait d'utiliser du rouge à la place du vert sur l'emballage d'une marque de pain a complètement tué le produit. Pour le cerveau, la couleur verte associée à du pain signifie moisissure, ce qui explique que les consommateurs ont d'instinct évité la marque. Avant même de vérifier la date de consommation du produit, les clients l'ont écarté en une fraction de seconde.

L'équipe chargée du branding d'une enseigne de vente à emporter devra non seulement analyser le marché et la concurrence, mais aussi et surtout, étudier la manière don le cerveau traite les informations relatives à la nourriture. Quelles sont les associations de couleurs qui sont agréables et « comestibles » et lesquelles sont à éviter ? Quelles matières suggèrent que le produit est organique ou naturel et pourquoi ? Quelles formes et images sont positives et quelles sont celles qui déclencheront le mode panique au niveau du cerveau et de l'instinct du consommateur ?

En plus des principes universels régissant la conception de marque, il est indispensable de prendre en compte le contexte local. En effet, un design ou un nom de produit perçu comme agréable et attirant dans un endroit donné pourra provoquer la réaction inverse ailleurs. Lorsque l'on développe ou adapte un concept pour une autre région, il faut impérativement analyser le contexte culturel local.

Enfin, la fonctionnalité des articles à emporter revêt également une importance capitale. Toute entreprise doit se demander si le packaging accompagnant son produit est vraiment bien conçu pour celui-ci. Le café ne risque-t-il pas de déborder au moment de retirer le couvercle s'il est trop ajusté ? Le contenu du sachet va-t-il se répandre partout s'il est trop difficile à ouvrir, obligeant le client à forcer ? Si l'on pose le produit sur la table, reste-t-il bien droit ? Le carton aura-t-il tendance à absorber l'humidité s'il est gardé trop longtemps en stock ou se détrempera-t-il sous l'effet de la condensation s'il est chauffé au four à micro-ondes ? Et enfin, comment l'éliminer une fois qu'il aura rempli son office ?

Tous les jours, des milliers de designers et d'agences de par le monde travaillent sur ces questions, et des centaines d'autres. Le présent ouvrage vous ouvre les portes de leur fascinant univers et vous dévoile les problèmes qu'ils ont à résoudre au quotidien et les solutions créatives qu'ils ont su trouver.

Puisque j'ai sauté mon petit-déjeuner ce matin, il est temps que j'aille au café du coin commander quelque chose...

DANIL SNITKO

DIRECTOR DE ARTE DE LA AGENCIA DE BRANDING PUNK YOU BRANDS
WWW.PUNK-YOU.RU

Te levantas de la cama por la mañana con los ojos entrecerrados; mientras estabas medio dormido habías puesto la función repetición de alarma, y ahora das saltos sobre una pierna por el piso poniéndote la ropa y recogiendo tus cosas para ir al trabajo. Ni pensar en desayunar. Ya ni te acuerdas de la última vez que tuviste tiempo de tomarte una taza de café antes de entrar a trabajar por la mañana. «Quizá pueda parar en una cafetería y llevarme un café y algo de comer», te dices. Es, más o menos, la misma idea que pasa todos los días por las mentes de millones de habitantes de la ciudad.

Los restaurantes y otros establecimentos de comida que ofrecen productos para llevar están ganando más clientes cada vez, y esto se nota especialmente en las grandes áreas metropolitanas, donde la gente debe apresurarse y hacer transbordos para llegar a su destino. Ya no tenemos tiempo para ir paseando, dedicar un buen rato al almuerzo o sentarnos a tomar un café.

La creciente competencia y las nuevas formas de comunicación con el cliente requieren un enfoque completamente diferente de la creación de marca en este sector. Las opciones de diseño de marca ya no se limitan a la creación de rótulos y de menús: deben atraer la atención del cliente en medio del torbellino que envuelve continuamente la vida de las personas que viven en la gran ciudad.

El diseño del packaging de los productos para llevar también es muy importante. El branding de los establecimientos de *takeaway* es diferente del de los restaurantes clásicos y gira en torno a una serie distinta de cuestiones. Para atraer la atención del consumidor tiene que ser extraordinario, pero no demasiado excéntrico, ya que, en general, el cliente se comerá la comida directamente del envase, es decir, del packaging.

Los humanos somos criaturas emotivas. Buscamos cada día nuevos sentimientos y experiencias, incluso aunque esta necesidad no sea tan apremiante como la sensación de hambre. Por ello, no es sorprendente que las marcas con un diseño profundamente emocional se estén haciendo populares. La compra de comida y bebida para llevar es un proceso espontáneo en el cual la toma de decisiones se rige por las emociones del cliente.

Además, hay que tener en cuenta el hecho de que la búsqueda de comida es uno de los instintos básicos de supervivencia. Cualquier información relacionada con la comida es analizada en una zona de nuestro cerebro que fue programada hace millones de años. Antes de que decidamos de manera consciente si queremos o no ese bocado, nuestro cerebro ya sabe que no vamos a comérnoslo porque huele mal o tiene mal aspecto. ¿Qué tiene de malo exactamente? «No lo sé, pero créeme: no te conviene», nos dice esa antiquísima zona de nuestro cerebro; y nosotros le hacemos caso porque desobedecerla podría costarnos caro. Hay que reconocer que después de millones de años nuestro cerebro sigue siendo muy eficaz cuando se trata de saber qué alimentos podemos o no comer.

Así pues, el diseño de todo lo relacionado con la comida –ya sea el de packaging o el de branding de restaurantes– se enfrenta a algunos difíciles retos. La parte primitiva de nuestro cerebro lo analiza para decidir si es comestible o no. Por eso en este sector, como en tantos otros, el diseñador o la agencia tienen siempre gran parte de la responsabilidad de los resultados. Un movimiento en falso, un error de juicio, pueden conducir a un fracaso comercial. Por ejemplo, en una ocasión, el cambio del color de la etiqueta de un pan de rojo a verde acabó literalmente con la marca. Resultó que el color verde en una rebanada de pan fue percibido como moho, lo cual disparó las alarmas del cerebro y los instintos, que avisaron a los clientes de que sería mejor evitar aquel pan. Incluso antes de mirar la fecha de caducidad, el diseño provocó el rechazo hacia el pan en un milisegundo.

Para trabajar en el branding de un establecimiento de comida takeaway, el equipo de diseño debe investigar no sólo el mercado y la competencia sino también, y más importante, el modo en que el cerebro analiza la información sobre la comida. ¿Qué combinaciones de color parecen agradables y *comestibles* y cuáles no? ¿Qué materiales sugieren que el producto es orgánico y natural y por qué? ¿Cómo interactuará el cliente con el producto? ¿Qué formas e imágenes son adecuadas y qué otras pondrán el cerebro y los instintos del cliente en *modo pánico*?

Además de los principios universales de evaluación del diseño, es esencial tener en cuenta el contexto cultural local. Un diseño o el nombre de un producto que se perciba claramente como agradable en un sitio puede provocar exactamente la reacción opuesta en otro. Siempre que se desarrolla o se adapta un diseño a una nueva región es necesario llevar a cabo un estudio del contexto cultural local.

Por último, la funcionalidad es extremadamente importante cuando se trata de *takeaway*. Una empresa puede tener ya un packaging para uno de sus productos, pero ¿será el adecuado para llevarlo? ¿Se derramará el café al levantar esa tapa demasiado apretada? ¿Se esparcirá por todas partes el contenido de un paquete porque el packaging está hecho de un material demasiado denso que obliga al consumidor a aplicar mucha fuerza al intentar abrirlo? Si ponemos el producto en una mesa, ¿se mantendrá en pie? ¿La cartulina se pondrá húmeda y pastosa por un almacenamiento prolongado o por la condensación al calentarla en el microondas? Y, finalmente, ¿puede desecharse el envase adecuadamente?

Miles de diseñadores y agencias de todo el mundo se ocupan cada día de todas estas cuestiones y de cientos de asuntos similares. Este libro nos introduce en su mundo y nos revela los enigmas a los que se enfrentan los diseñadores y las soluciones creativas que han encontrado trabajando en este campo fascinante.

Y ahora, como esta mañana he tenido que saltarme el desayuno, creo que es hora de irme y conseguir un café y algo de comer...

DANIL SNITKO

DIRETOR DE ARTE DA AGÊNCIA DE BRANDING PUNK YOU BRANDS
WWW.PUNK-YOU.RU

Você sai da cama de manhã com os olhos apertados; ainda meio adormecido, havia acionado a função soneca, e agora fica pulando numa perna só pelo apartamento enquanto se veste e junta as coisas para sair para o trabalho. Não dá nem para pensar em tomar o café da manhã. Você já nem se lembra de quando foi a última vez em que teve tempo de tomar uma xícara de café antes de entrar no trabalho de manhã. "Talvez eu possa parar numa cafeteria e levar um café e alguma coisa para comer", diz a si mesmo. É, mais ou menos, essa mesma ideia que, todos os dias, passa pela cabeça de milhões de habitantes da cidade.

Os restaurantes e outros estabelecimentos de alimentação que fornecem produtos para viagem estão ganhando cada vez clientes, e isto se nota especialmente nas grandes áreas metropolitanas, onde as pessoas precisam se apressar e tomar mais de um meio de transporte para chegar ao seu destino. Já não temos tempo para ir passeando, para ter um bom intervalo para o almoço ou para tomar um café.

A concorrência crescente e as novas formas de comunicação com o cliente requerem um enfoque completamente diferente da criação de uma marca neste setor. As opções de design de marca já não podem limitar-se à criação de rótulos e de menus: precisam chamar a atenção do cliente no meio do turbilhão que envolve continuamente a vida das pessoas que vivem na grande cidade.

O design do packaging dos produtos para viagem também é muito importante. O branding dos estabelecimentos de *takeaway* é diferente do dos restaurantes clássicos e gira em torno de uma série de questões bem diferentes. Para conseguir chamar a atenção do consumidor ele precisa ser extraordinário, mas não demasiadamente excêntrico, pois, em geral, o cliente comerá o alimento diretamente da embalagem, ou seja, do packaging.

Os seres humanos somos criaturas emotivas. Buscamos a cada dia novos sentimentos e experiências, mesmo que esta necessidade não seja tão premente como a sensação de fome. Por isso, não é de surpreender que as marcas com um design profundamente emocional tenham se tornado tão populares. A compra de alimentos e bebidas para viagem é um processo espontâneo, no qual a tomada de decisões é ditada pelas emoções do cliente.

Além disso, é preciso levar em conta o fato de que a busca de alimento seja um dos instintos básicos de sobrevivência. Qualquer informação relacionada com a comida é analisada numa zona do nosso cérebro que foi programada há milhões de anos. Antes que nós possamos decidir de maneira consciente se queremos ou não este bocado, o nosso cérebro já sabe que não o comeremos porque cheira mal ou porque tem um aspecto ruim. O que ele tem de ruim, exatamente? "Não sei, mas pode acreditar: não é bom para você", é o que nos diz essa antiquíssima zona do nosso cérebro; e nós lhe obedecemos porque desobedecê-la poderia custar-nos muito caro. É preciso reconhecer que, depois de milhões de anos, o nosso cérebro continua sendo muito eficiente quando se trata de saber que alimentos nós podemos ou não comer.

Deste modo, o design de tudo o que se relaciona com a comida – quer seja o packaging ou branding de restaurantes– depara-se com alguns difíceis desafios. A parte primitiva do nosso cérebro o analisa para decidir se é comestível ou não. Por isso, neste setor, como em tantos outros, o designer ou a agência têm sempre uma grande parte da responsabilidade pelos resultados. Um movimento em falso, um erro de avaliação, podem levar a um fracasso comercial. Por exemplo, em certa ocasião, a mudança da cor, de vermelha para verde, da etiqueta de um pão literalmente acabou com a marca. Aconteceu que a cor verde numa rabanada de pão foi interpretada como mofo, e isso disparou os alarmes do cérebro e dos instintos, que avisaram os clientes que seria melhor evitar aquele pão. Antes mesmo de olhar a data de vencimento, o design provocou a rejeição do pão num milissegundo.

Para trabalhar no branding de um estabelecimento de alimentação takeaway, a equipe de design deve pesquisar não só o mercado e a concorrência, mas também, e principalmente, o modo como o cérebro analisa a informação sobre o alimento. Que combinações de cor parecem agradáveis e *comestíveis* e quais não? Que materiais sugerem que o produto é orgânico e natural e por que? Como o cliente vai interagir com o produto? Que formas e imagens serão adequadas e que outras colocarão o cérebro e os instintos do cliente em *modo de pânico*?

Além dos princípios universais de avaliação do design, é essencial levar em conta o contexto cultural local. Um design ou o nome de um produto que seja captado claramente como agradável num lugar pode provocar a reação exatamente oposta em outro. Sempre que se desenvolve ou se adapta um design para uma nova região, é necessário realizar um estudo do contexto cultural local.

Por fim, a funcionalidade é extremamente importante no caso do takeaway. Uma empresa pode já ter um packaging para um dos seus produtos, porém será que ele é adequado para transportar? Será que o café se derramará ao levantar-se esta tampa apertada demais? Será que o conteúdo de um pacote se espalhará por todo lado porque o packaging foi feito com um material muito denso, obrigando o consumidor a fazer muita força ao tentar abri-lo? Se colocarmos o produto numa mesa, ele se manterá em pé? O papel do invólucro ficará úmido e pastoso devido a um armazenamento prolongado ou à condensação ao ser aquecido no microondas? E, finalmente, é possível descartar adequadamente o invólucro?

Milhares de designers e de agências de todo o mundo se dedicam a responder diariamente a todas essas questões e a centenas de assuntos similares. Este livro introduz-nos em seu mundo e nos revela os enigmas que os designers enfrentam e as soluções criativas que encontraram ao trabalhar neste campo fascinante.

E agora, como nesta manhã eu tive que pular o café da manhã, creio que é hora de tentar conseguir um café e alguma coisa para comer...

SAUCE RESTAURANT

AGENCY: MARTY WEISS AND FRIENDS **CREATIVE DIRECTION**: MARTY WEISS **DESIGN**: ANDREA D'AQUINO, EULIE LEE

"Sauce" is Chef Frank Prisinzano's 4th restaurant, joining Frank, Lil' Frankies and Supper. Following in the foot-steps of Frank's other restaurants, Sauce is warm, authentic, with an almost undesigned design esthetic. The identity by Marty Weiss and Friends, featuring pots, pigs and cows hovering over grandmotherly wallpaper, mixes the old world vision of Frank and partner Rob De Florio with a quirky modern spin. The Allen Street storefront is the entrance for the grocery and butcher shop, as well as the restaurant. For the typography and design, they drew inspiration from old New York Italian Pork and Grocery storefronts.

PIKKEN BISTRO & BAKERY

DESIGN: MAK YU JING, EUDORA KOH WEN YI, GERALDINE PECK, WONG JUN YI

Pikken Bistro & Bakery is a fresh and cheerful cafe located in sunny island, Singapore. Drop by for a nice cuppa in the morning, sit down for a nice quiet lunch or immerse yourself in great music from the live bands under the starry sky. The bistro is run by a quartet who has a passion and flair for Arts & Design, while at the same time having strong interest in gastronomy. They aim to serve the best quality food with quality service to create a homely atmosphere. Pikken is definitely the place you'd want to visit with a friend or two over a cup of coffee.

BOUCH

AGENCY: FIRMALT **DESIGN:** MANUEL LLAGUNO

Bouch Burger Bistro was created with the intent of perfecting the burger. Each burger has been carefully crafted to provide a unique and thoroughly enjoyable flavor. The burger is created from the ground up, which means the bread, sauces and spices are made in-house to guarantee quality.
The concept is inspired by small specialty butcher shops, where products are hand-picked to ensure the finest and freshest selection for their clients. It was important for the brand to represent quality products.
The packaging was designed having in mind that it had to be practical for transport, easy to use, and cost-effective.

VESUVIO PIZZERIA

DESIGN: ANGELICA BAINI

This was a university project. Angelica created a fictional pizzeria based on Mount Vesuvius which is an active volcano that lies in Naples, Italy, known to have the greatest tasting tomatoes to grow from that soil. The technique of marbling helped portray lava and pizza for her concept. The creation of the logo sprung from those things and the packaging, itself.

KIGO KITCHEN

EXECUTIVE CREATIVE DIRECTION: JIM HAVEN **CREATIVE DIRECTION**: CLARA MULLIGAN, STEVE CULLEN **DESIGN**: CLARA MULLIGAN, STEVE CULLEN, JORDAN RUNDLE **PROJECT MANAGEMENT**: KATE RATLIFFE, JESSICA HARDY **PRODUCER**: STACY MCCANN **PRODUCTION DESIGN**: KIRY LUC, SACHA PAUL

Food is a way to experience adventure. Taste buds can take you places you have never been before — they can take you off the beaten path and make us feel changed, fueled and fired up.

Kigo Kitchen is inspired by such adventure found in the back alleys of the Pan-Pacific where some of the world's best street food is found, with a healthy dose of frenetic energy on the side. The brand is loud, bold and layered, referencing the fast and repetitious nature of being an alley chef. The bold, brushed type honors the hand-crafted quick-fire bowl and straight-forward messaging reflects communication on the kitchen line. By combining the exotic soul of Pan-Asian street food, with simple touches of American style, the designers created a curious, dynamic, and flavorful experience.

DREUX & GHISALLO

DESIGN: JOHN WEGMAN **BRANDING ASSISTANT**: DAVID WEGMAN

Branding, stationery and packaging for a mobile coffee-vending tricycle. The brand revolves around the patron saint of coffee, Saint Dreux, and the patron saint of cycling, Madonna del Ghisallo. It is the intersection of Dreux and Ghisallo that is explored in the customized ampersand found in the logo.

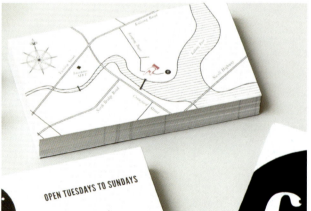

LOYSEL'S TOY

AGENCY: FOREIGN POLICY DESIGN GROUP **DESIGN:** YAH-LENG YU **DESIGN PRODUCTION:** TIANYU ISAIAH ZHENG (TY) **ILLUSTRATION:** CHERYL CHONG

The look and feel is inspired by the signage of the traditional mom & pop grocery/produce stores and the farmers' markets. These places offer produce that are the freshest, possibly the most ecologically-friendly, direct from the local farmers and everything hand-prepared, hand-crafted. Nothing too fancy. Down to earth. Honest. Authentic. That ties in nicely with the ideals and philosophy of Loysel's Toy which have led the designer to coin the well-deserved tag for them – THE COFFEE CRAFTERS.

FIKA

AGENCY: DESIGNERS ANONYMOUS

Fika is named after the Swedish word for coffee break and Designers Anonymous needed no encouragement to express its 'Take a Break' proposition in a way that matches the brand's quirky personality and cosmopolitan location. Their branding solution is based on the notion of a break from the dull routine of daily life. This is subtly expressed by perforating sections around and within a mix of photographs and illustrations. Sections are perforated and removed and either assembled as collage or used individually to express a variety of messages. The perforated edging detail links each image back to Fika and the theme of 'Take a Break'.

ALL WORK
AND NO FIKA
MAKES ONE
A DULL HORSE.

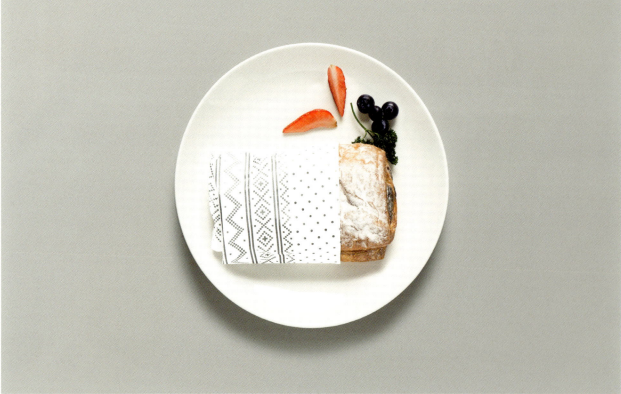

GALO KITCHEN

AGENCY: ANAGRAMA

Galo Kitchen is a restaurant specializing in French-American inspired comfort cuisine. Its prime focus is breakfast, but it also offers lunch and dinner menus and a cozy atmosphere all day long. Additionally, Galo Kitchen has its own in-house bakery that provides delicious, freshly made, handcrafted bread and pastries.

The naming is meant to articulate the French touch present in Galo's lovingly made food. The black and white skewed pattern dresses up the brand as friendly, snug and casual, a feeling supported by the logotype's organic cursive script. The zeppelin icon pays homage to Galo's bakery. Inspired on the airship's general shape, a zeppelin is a sandwich made with a roll of French bread split widthwise into two pieces and filled with a variety of meats, cheese, vegetables, seasonings and sauces.

HABIBIS

AGENCY: ANAGRAMA **PHOTOGRAPHY:** CAROGA

Habibis is an Arabic-Mexican fusion taqueria located in San Pedro Garza García, a city enriched by the culinary treats of its third generation Arab immigrants. Previously a humble taco stand, Habibis approached Anagrama with the task of creating a brand that communicated the foods' exceptional mixed background and quality without losing its street-friendly and casual demeanor.

Anagrama's proposal is a brand that adapts stylized Arabic calligraphy to a typical Mexican street setting, complete with neon colors and inexpensive materials, like craft paper bags. Deep research and careful understanding of the Arabic alphabet was needed to design, using calligraphic pens and special brushes, the various words and signage in both Arabic and Latin. The custom type is accompanied by Gotham, a gentle and neutral typeface that would allow the bespoken logotypes to stand out above everything else. The pattern is based on traditional keffiyeh (a Middle Eastern headdress fashioned from a square scarf) and gorgeously intrinsic mosaic patterns.

UPTOWN 966

AGENCY: WONDEREIGHT **CREATIVE DIRECTION:** WALID NASRALA, KARIM ABOURIZK **ART DIRECTION:** KARIM ABOURIZK, LEA HESHME
DESIGN: LEA HESHME **PHOTOGRAPHY:** KARIM ABOURIZK

The client came to WonderEight for help in creating a new concept in a star location in KSA.
The location used to host a winning concept with a success story in the area, and this was the challenge they were excited to take: Gaining client's
acceptance with expectations already set to "high" although the offering was the same as the previous concept, they created a completely new experience
that leaves you with a familiar feeling at the end of your visit.

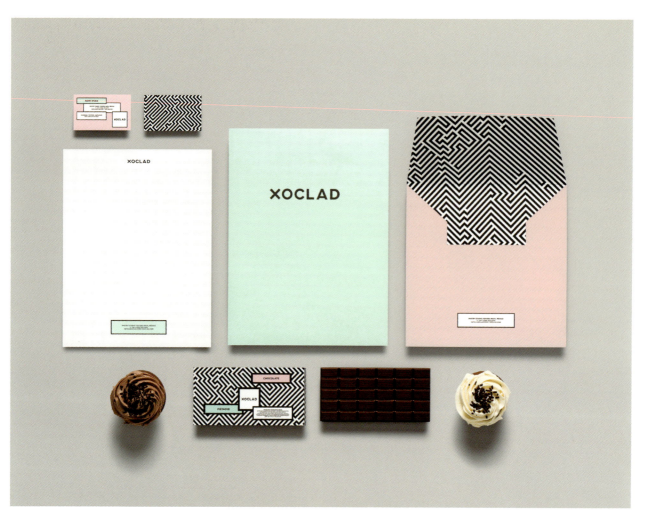

XOCLAD

AGENCY: ANAGRAMA

Xoclad is a high-end pastry and confectionery shop located in the Mayan Riviera. In a place bustling with tourist activity, Xoclad needed to communicate the area's strong Mayan culture in a classy way that could never be called cliché or tacky.
First, Anagrama gave its name a visual and phonetic pre-hispanic feeling that also conveyed one of the shop's prime products: chocolate. Then they designed a labyrinth-like pattern reminiscent of antique Mayan art and architecture ornamentation. The color palette consigns the brand with a sober, clean feeling that makes it modern and sweet.

DEAR JOE

AGENCY: GARBERGS PROJECT **DESIGN**: KARIN AHLGREN **FINAL ART**: JOHANNA HERLIN, JONAS BÄCKMAN **COPYWRITING**: PER FORSSBERG, SARAH SNAVELY **ACCOUNT DIRECTION**: ÅSA BERG **ACCOUNT MANAGER**: DANIELLA DZIJAN **ASSISTANT**: MIKAEL BEVENTORP

Name and visual identity for a new frozen yogurt brand.
Featuring a personal note addressed to you, a white background, classic typography and color splashes as the different "flavors", the identity tells the story of a healthier, more natural and more honest frozen yogurt. With the cherry on top, it has been named the tastiest frozen yogurt in Sweden.

SANTA CRUZ

AGENCY: ANAGRAMA **PHOTOGRAPHY:** CAROGA (FOR ALL BRANDING PICS), JUMA (FOR ALL RESTAURANT PICS) **ARCHITECT:** EIJI HAYAKAWA

Santa Cruz is a quick service Mexican BBQ restaurant located in Santa Catarina, a municipality of the greater Monterrey area in northeast Mexico. Santa Cruz's menu contains food such as brisket and baby-back ribs slow-cooked to tender perfection and offered in an array of different ready-to-go, conventional styles such as burgers and tacos.

The hand-made quality of the logotype and overall identity is meant to praise the careful, traditional and apprehensive food making process of Santa Cruz. The brand is simple and direct, and above all, always honest and sincere, never attempting to hide its conceptual rugged awkwardness. Destined to be franchised in the future, Santa Cruz's honest and handcrafted demeanor will inevitably be distinctive amid all other, more synthetic fast food chain restaurants.

The project was done in collaboration with architect Eiji Hayakawa. While Anagrama developed the brand values and visual identity, Eiji worked on the restaurant's unique and unusual architecture. The massive, scarlet barn-like structure is distinctively prominent amid the industrially gray and blue mountainous backdrop of its physical setting.

ASCHAN DELI

AGENCY: BOND CREATIVE AGENCY **DESIGN:** ALEKSI HAUTAMÄKI, TUUKKA KOIVISTO, JANNE NOROKYTÖ **PHOTOGRAPHY:** PAAVO LEHTONEN

Aschan Deli is an urban quick stop for breakfast, lunch, snack or coffee. The aim was to create a concept that looks fresh and modern while communicating convenience. The symbols, used in the signage, communications and interior, are a big part of the identity. Bright colours were introduced to bring more life and sparkle into the interior.

ASCHAN
DELI

	2,50
	3,00
KAHVI/COFFEE	3,20
ESPRESSO	4,50
CAFÉ MACCHIATO	3,50
LATTE MACCHIATO	3,50
AMERICANO	

FLOCK CAFÉ

AGENCY: KILO STUDIO **CREATIVE DIRECTION:** BENJY CHOO **DESIGN:** JERVIC TAN, LU JIAYI, ANGELA THNG

Flock Café is a family run establishment that prides itself in freshly made all-day breakfasts and artisanal coffee. The brand is built upon the concept of "Coming Together", assembled primarily using various unique patterns representing different parts of the café.

This allowed Kilo Studio to extend the concept into multiple types of livery such as badges, hand screened aprons and cup sleeves. Most notable would be the namecards, which would be comprised of 3 different designs that would form a larger pattern when pieced together.

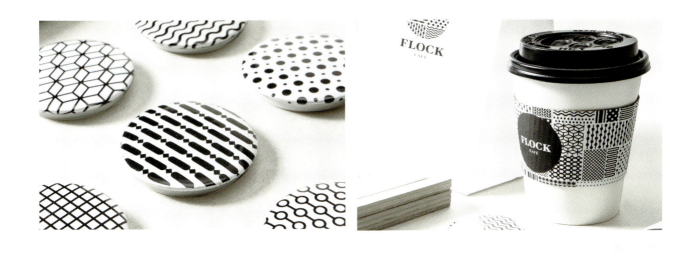

PROVISIONS

AGENCY: FOREIGN POLICY DESIGN GROUP **DESIGN:** YAH-LENG YU

Provisions functions as the retail & take-out section of two adjacent restaurants within a residential complex. It is really a mom & pop deli/grocery/sundries store inspired by the Australian milk bar/grocery from the good o'days, where transportation were horses with horse carriages and maybe the railway, and where outposts/depots were the places to get mails, wares & basic supplies. Supplies come in galvanized cans, basic brown bags, crates and sacks.

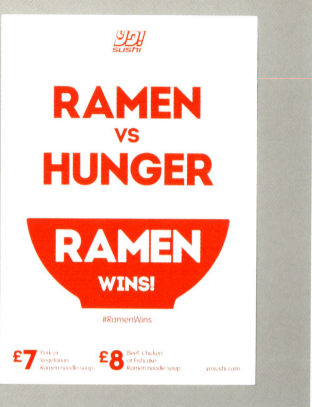

YO! SUSHI RAMEN VS HUNGER

AGENCY: KENTLYONS

KentLyons was commissioned by YO! Sushi to create a campaign to promote their new range of large Ramen dishes for both in-store and takeaway. KentLyons created a fully integrated campaign for launch, including TV and online viral adverts, in-store branding, takeaway packaging, T-shirts, outdoor and press advertising, menus as well as a series of viral videos to support the campaign, featuring wearable giant Ramen takeaway pots creating havoc. All these helped to sell 100,000 bowls of YO! Sushi Ramen in 4 weeks.

CROSTINI BAKERY & CAFÉ

AGENCY: BOX BRAND DESIGN LIMITED **ART DIRECTION:** YVONNE CHUNG **DESIGN/ILLUSTRATION:** JOEY LO, JY. CHEN

Picturing a view that riding a bicycle across the streets in France, Box Brand Design Limited created the brand image of "Crostini", a bakery with a light touch of French ambience. They depict a nostalgic bicycle sketch as the brand's main image. Following the style, they extend to various visual images along with the royal blue and gold color system and apply to the store appearance and packages. The visual images and exquisite Crostini products together create a new consistent brand.

THE YOGURT SHOP

DESIGN: LOUISE SKAFTE

The yogurt shop is a small yogurt bar located in Copenhagen, Denmark. It's owned and operated by Marile Krogh and Christiana Wiboltt. They created the idea through their own love of food, relationship with people and overall wellbeing.

The main idea behind the design was an aim to create an identity with limited colour palette, clean typography and simple shapes. Then finished it up with a touch of femininity and easily recognizable references to the Nordic style.

Each aspect of the shop has been handpicked from high quality and organic Danish suppliers. This has been reflected in every aspect of the identity of the brand, enhancing your experience and relationship with it.

It was also important to make it a part of iconic Nordic design so it could be easily expanded over Scandinavia.

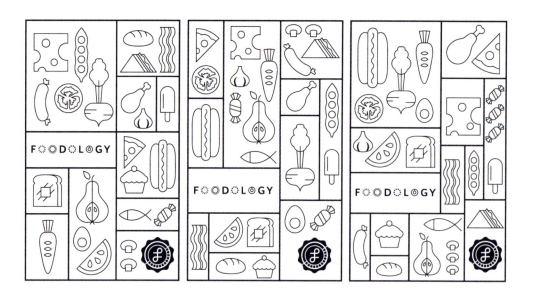

FOODOLOGY

PASTA

PIZZA

BURGERS & GRILL

SANDWICH (WESTERN)

ASIAN NOODLES

ASIAN SANDWICHES

ASIAN RICE WITH SIDES

BAR

DESSERT

SALAD

SOUP

GRAB & GO

FOODOLOGY

AGENCY: SOMEWHERE ELSE

Based on the name, the identity treats Foodology as an institution for food and borrows different graphic elements from academia to create its own unique voice. To ensure that the identity system is flexible enough to accommodate the different situations and broad spectrum of applications such a brand may encounter, an extensive set of illustrations and secondary graphics were also developed. These graphics allow the brand to be dynamic and show customers a multi-faceted, well rounded personality.

DOLCE BAKERY

AGENCY: STIR AND ENJOY **CREATIVE DIRECTION/COPYWRITING:** BRENT ANDERSON **DESIGN:** SARAH NELSEN

Dolce Baking Co. was 5 years old and well-known but the owner felt her branding didn't match up to her baked goods or her vision for the company. Stir and Enjoy helped Dolce divine the true essence of the business and how to elevate it. The name was tweaked to a more friendly and familiar Dolce Bakery. The new logo, color palette and design arsenal now embody the business' philosophy: Signature twists on bakery classics. Stir and Enjoy also gave new life to existing packaging materials through rubber stamps, multiple patterns and a vibrant, coordinated set of stickers.

FISH N CAKE

DESIGN: EGGPLANT FACTORY

Fish n Cake is a fish cake store located in Seoul, South Korea. Fish cake is a common street food along with Topokki (Korean snack food made from soft rice cake and sweet spicy sauce). However, Fish n Cake wanted to sell fish cake as a side dish of a meal and for quality gift. At Fish n Cake store, customers can purchase quality fish cakes for side dish and gift set. Eggplant Factory designed various packages for Fish n Cake while maintaining their current brand identity. They suggested the client to sell heart-warming take-out fish cakes with take-out coffee cups.

보기 좋은 어묵이 먹기도 좋다.

KORODON
DESIGN: EGGPLANT FACTORY

Korodon is a korokke (Japanese croquette) & tonkatsu take-out café. Korokke is a popular street food in Korea. Usually, take-out korokkes are wrapped with square-shaped waxed paper, and packed in a paper bag. Eggplant Factory wanted to position korokke as "giftable" food. For Korodons take-out package, korokkes are wrapped with cone-shaped waxed paper, and then packed in a swiss roll cake box, which is suitable for gift as well.

FUJIYAMA COOKIE

AGENCY: FROM GRAPHIC **CREATIVE DIRECTION:** MYU PLANNING & OPERATORS INC. **ART DIRECTION/DESIGN:** YOKO MARUYAMA **PHOTOGRAPHY:** ATSUSHI MAYA, YOSHIFUMI IKEDA

Fujiyama Cookie is a cookie shop near Lake Kawaguchi on the foot of Mt. Fuji. FROM GRAPHIC used the typography to design the logo by mixing Japanese brush painting and Western-style calligraphy. The unique logo, which is based on the cookie's shape of Mt. Fuji, also looks like a face. For a package of three or five cookies, they made them in a different shape of Mt. Fuji based on a motif. To introduce the taste of freshly baked cookies, all of the packages are transparent so that their customers can see the cookies before opening the packages.

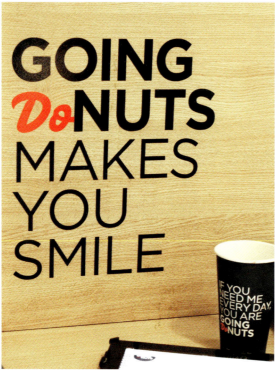

GOING DONUTS

AGENCY: FARMGROUP **CREATIVE/ART DIRECTION:** TAP KRUAVANICHKIT **DESIGN:** JIJIRA DASANANJALI, POOMRUETHAI SUEBSANTIWONGSE, KRITTI KUHARUANGRONG **PHOTOGRAPHY:** BUAKAEW C. SIMMELKJAER

Branding + Identity Design + Package Design + Retail Design for An original American donut shop in Herning, Denmark.
The name of the shop was given to Farmgroup by the client and they found that the name "Going Donuts" is super interesting and has so much character inside it already. So they decided to play with typographic pun. They wanted to make it their core idea of the brand and everything would spin off that main idea. As you can see, they've tried to create the whole identity and branding system around it. The team tried to be sarcastic and even bitchy sometimes just to really express the sense of humor and fun. They really wanted it to be witty, simple, fun and something that makes people smile.
Since it's an American donut shop, located in Denmark, branded and designed in Thailand, Farmgroup found this very ironic. So the first thing they've proposed to client is the big wall typography says "Americans are Going (Do) Nuts" and across the wall they proposed "Scandinavians are Going (Do) Nuts". Client thought it was too bold, so the team finally went with just "Hi there! It's alright if you're Going (Do) Nuts." It wasn't as sarcastic as they wanted it to be, but they were very happy that client bought their idea. Once this is decided, the rest were pretty easy to carry everything through the whole identity system.

BEIJING8

AGENCY: GARBERGS PROJECT **DESIGN:** KARIN AHLGREN **FINAL ART:** BEATRICE SZTANSKA **ACCOUNT MANAGER:** CHARLOTTE LUNDQUIST, ANNA OHLSSON

A complete visual identity ranging from logotype and interior design to take-away packaging and clothing. Garbergs Project combine the ancient Chinese food culture with young, Scandinavian values of ecology and sustainability, while also reflecting "slow fast food".
The design idea mixes the clean, Nordic style with the colorful Chinese style. They do this by using plain, straightforward, recycled materials with small details in bright color. The quality of the food served is reflected in the craftsmanship and details of the design. To keep the design up to date they change the staff T-shirt every Chinese New Year, according to the Chinese zodiac.

PIE & ALE HOUSE

DESIGN: BAGS OF JOY

Proposed design for pop up Pie & Ale stall in London.

MÃOS DE MANTEIGA

DESIGN: DAVID SANTOS, JOANA SANTOS, JOSÉ ARAÚJO, MARGARIDA MOUTA, MARIA BRANCO

Mãos De Manteiga was developed as an academic project for the class of Strategic Design, taught by Prof. Álvaro Sousa at Universidade de Aveiro as part of the last year of the Design Degree. The students were required to come up with a concept, identity and strategy for a fictional fast-food restaurant. The concept behind Mãos de Manteiga (literally "butter hands") is a brunch/pancake restaurant that encourages clients to eat with their hands and dismiss the flatware.

EMBUTIQUE

EMBUTIQUE

AGENCY: DUCXE | STUDIO **ART DIRECTION:** XABIER OGANDO, BEATRIZ PEIXOTO

Brand design and take-away packaging for a Spanish food company in London. The tradition of Spanish products fuses with a London "hipster" touch. The font and illustrations represent the distinctive identity of the brand.

BAKER & MORE

AGENCY: WONDEREIGHT **CREATIVE DIRECTION:** WALID NASRALA, KARIM ABOURIZK **ART DIRECTION/DESIGN/PHOTOGRAPHY:** KARIM ABOURIZK

WonderEight were asked to create the identity of a new coffee shop in town serving delicious buns, signature coffee, tea, macaroons and breakfast. The main challenge was to make Baker & More stand out in a wide range of commercial coffee shops and to attract a different, higher class of customers. The results were a trendy yet classy looking coffee shop. They focused on the materials used rather on the graphic visuals, like jute/burlap bags, wooden containers, nice tableware, etc. to help convey the unicity and genuineness of the place.

GALOMOS

AGENCY: DUCXE | STUDIO **ART DIRECTION**: XABIER OGANDO, BEATRIZ PEIXOTO

Design of brand and take-away packaging of new nuggets. The result comes from the wish of increasing the value of the Galician native products through a useful and modern offer. The image communicates ethnic and cultural values of the home area.

NADOMURA

DESIGN: PUNK YOU BRANDS

The brand identity is designed to be noticeable to the consumers and to carry the key message — Nadomura's Japanese food is so fresh, that is almost alive. After all, the main advantage, that distinguishes the company from its competitors, is an innovative packaging. Hermetically packed up sushi are delivered to the consumer in its original form — the most fresh form. An octopus printed on the packages is, obviously, too fresh.

ON THE WOK

ART DRECTION/DESIGN: OSCAR BASTIDAS **ILLUSTRATION:** OSCAR BASTIDAS **PHOTOGRAPHY:** ALVARO CAMACHO

On the Wok is an Asian fast food concept restaurant located in Caracas - Venezuela, focused on noodles to take away. A fusion between Asian icons and Occidental graphic style set all the inspiration of the restaurant's visual concept, using only 3 colors to consolidate the atmosphere of the restaurant: yellow, red and woody brown.

AREA FOUR

AGENCY: KORN DESIGN **CREATIVE DIRECTION:** DENISE KORN **ART DIRECTION/DESIGN:** JESHURUN WEBB **DESIGN SUPPORT:** MAX FISHER

Area Four is a fast-paced, high energy restaurant with a commitment to local and sustainable sourcing, as well as unpretentious hospitality. They are known for never taking shortcuts – serving pizza dough that is fermented for 30 hours, homemade mozzarella, house-butchered meat, house-baked pastries, and perfectly extracted espresso shots.

The new branding for Area Four communicates the same energy and hand-crafted approach that has come to define their cuisine and overall philosophy. This unconventional utilitarian branding was highly influenced by the music-loving, youthful energy of its two owners. Hip, rough, and full of punk, this new system was deployed across new menus, packaging, branded items and signage. It is integrated throughout the Coffee, Bakery, Pizza, Food Truck and Catering arms of the business.

L'ENCANT

AGENCY: CAN CUN **DESIGN:** NÚRIA VILA **PHOTOGRAPHY:** ANNA RIGAU

Located in the city center of Granollers, L'ENCANT is a place for having a drink, snack, lunch, dinner on the terrace or just taking the food back home at your convenience. The aim is to provide everyone with fresh, varied quality food at reasonable prices.

Can Cun wanted to create an image that they approach the world of sushi without forgetting the Catalan product. The apostrophe and the chopstick, the vertical writing and the letter can be fans as they are connecting the two cultures.

Menus are made of stone paper (cradle to cradle). They can be reused and modified that minimize the energy and resource cost.

MILK & HONEY

AGENCY: SEEMEDESIGN

Milk & Honey is a locally-owned breakfast, lunch, craft coffee and gelato shop in Chattanooga, Tennessee. High-quality, homemade and, most importantly, real – the Milk & Honey brand was a dream project in every sense of the word. It came to life first through the logo and printed collateral, moving into interior styling, signage, coffee sleeves, wall menus and murals, labels, packaging, freezer wraps, gelato carts, apparel and so much more. There is wit and warmth tucked into every nook and cranny. The combination of custom design, copy, illustration and type treatments creates a friendly feeling of community. The goal of the brand identity was to create a space where it's hard to feel anything but happiness when you walk through the door.

KAFFEE KANN ICH.

AGENCY: CYNTHIA WAEYUSOH COMMUNICATION DESIGN **DESIGN:** CYNTHIA WAEYUSOH **PHOTOGRAPHY:** FLORIAN BISON

Corporate Design for the German brand named "Kaffee kann ich." (I can make coffee). Only the finest locally grown ingredients are used. The choice products are marked and certified with the round brand label.

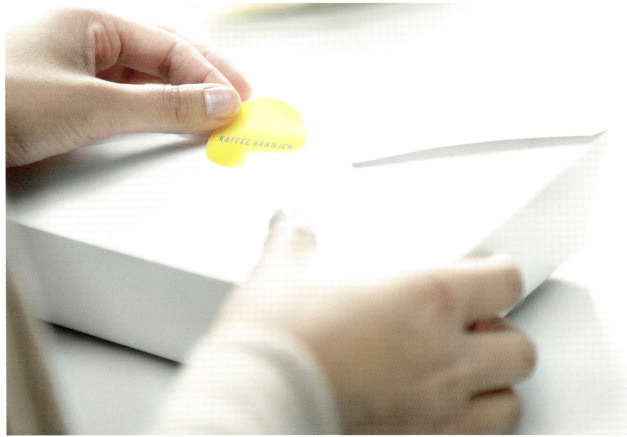

BAKER'S 12

DESIGN: ENAV TOMER **INSTRUCTION:** NURIT KONIAK

Baker's 12 is a student project of Shenkar College of Engineering and Design. Baker's Dozen, an urban lighthearted pastry shop, was designed with naive, clean illustrations, and humorous phrases.

baked goods.
daaamn good.

check out
that cupcake..

mmmm
doughnut

croissant
ooh la la

check out
that cupcake..

ÁLADE AIRLINES CÁTERIN

DESIGN: JORGE ATRESPUNTOS

Álade Airlines is a hypothetical airways company based on offering an entire experience before, and during the flight. The company individualizes the needs of each passenger to bring them a specific kind of flight.
Following the spirit of the company, Álade Airlines tries to offer a high quality catering service with some dishes inspired by Mediterranean diet. Using engravings and classical etchings, it mimics the tables for aristocracy during the XVII century.

DRINK BETTER WINE

DESIGN: CHARLOTTE FOSDIKE

Drink Better Wine is a cafe, restaurant and wine bar based in Sydney, Australia. The brief was to redesign their logo, stationery collateral, packaging and menus in an earthy, vintage, warm and inviting style. With this in mind, Charlotte Fosdike and her partners developed a pattern that consisted of hand painted wine bottles and other cooking utensils to make up a bold and interesting black and white pattern. They used brown papers to give the branding a natural and earthy feel and old style typography to give the designs that vintage look. As the take away branding was important to entice new customers to the shop, they designed a wine wrap, bag and label for the bottles and used this same wrap for the takeaway baked goods.

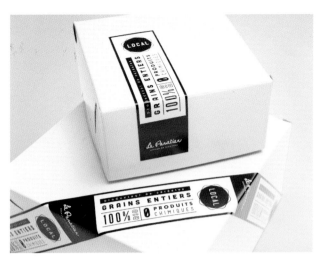

LE PANETIER

DESIGN: ANDRÉANNE TEASDALE, STÉPHANY MARTEL

Rebranding of Le Panetier, an organic artisanal bakery in Quebec city. The project was done for a graphic design class at Université Laval.

ELINA'S BAKERY

DESIGN: THE BIRTHDAYS™

Elina's Bakery is about a homemade sweets bakery. The design of the logo and applications, aim to communicate the most essential characteristic of the bakery, that is homemade, and also maintain a potential for growing a wider business in the future, with this characteristic being unchanged. Various applications have been designed such as take-away boxes, paper bags, poster, badges, stickers, wrapping paper and recipe books.

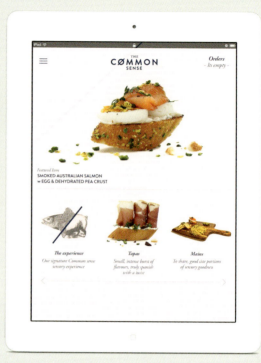

THE COMMON SENSE

DESIGN/ILLUSTRATION/CRAFT: SHERMAN CHIA J.W

The Common Sense is about taking the common expected ingredients, reinventing it and delivering it through a sensory experience.
The Common Sense is positioned as a contemporary high end tapas bar and restaurant located in Melbourne. They are all about taking traditional elements and adding their own modern unique twist. Dining to them is not just about the food; it's the experience.

SCHASTYE RESTAURANT

ART DIRECTION/DESIGN: IRINA SHIROKOVA

Schastye is a pastry and confectionery chain based in Moscow and Saint-Petersburg, Russia. It's like a small piece of true France in Russia. The word "Schaste" means happiness. Schastye's commitment to Happiness permeates through every facet of the brand: food, packaging, interior and employees. Schastye guests dazzle in an assortment of products for purchase. Any dish or dessert can be taken "to-go" in one of several "precious" packages. Items are packaged individually by hand.

Schastye has its unique features - post of happiness, old-fashioned taxophone, music of happiness and clothes. Everything can be bought in the Happy Shop.

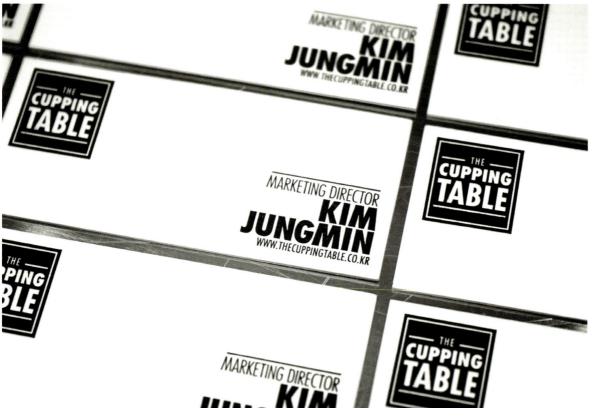

THE CUPPING TABLE

DESIGN: JUNGMIN KIM

Business planning, branding, and identity project of cafe The Cupping Table. Being in the country known with its second highest coffee consumption around the world, it has been a big challenge to set up a business model that can compete with franchise cafe brands. As existing brands focus on mass-consumption, Jungmin Kim has come up with a theme that can appeal to a smaller group of audience, who love authentic coffee culture as well as lifestyle and design.

MAKI-SAN

AGENCY: KINETIC SINGAPORE **CREATIVE DIRECTION:** PANN LIM **ART DIRECTION:** ESTHER GOH, ASTRI NURSALIM, GIAN JONATHAN, JACK TAN, PANN LIM **DESIGN:** ESTHER GOH, ASTRI NURSALIM, GIAN JONATHAN, JACK TAN **ILLUSTRATION:** ESTHER GOH **COPYWRITING:** EUGENE TAN, JOSEPH DAVIES **PROGRAMMER:** NOEL CHAN, BAGUS KUNCORO **ACCOUNT DIRECTOR:** DENNIS LIM

Kinetic Singapore was commissioned to work on the visual identity for a sushi store, who wanted to launch Singapore's first ever fully customizable sushi store. Being offered a wide selection of fresh ingredients, diners could pick and choose precisely what went into their hand-rolls.
Kinetic Singapore proposed naming the store "Maki-San" for one simple reason: the word "san" roughly translates as "mister" or "missus" in Japanese, and by using this suffix, each Maki could be uniquely personified. This idea also extends to operations: customers can name their own rolls however they choose to. The logo is made up of emoticons commonly used in Japanese pop culture.
Using hand-drawn illustrations of mushrooms, avocados, cucumbers, and other ingredients, Kinetic Singapore designed a myriad of patterns which became Maki-san's main visual identity. These motifs were applied throughout the consumer experience - right down to the packaging - to play up the endless, fun options available for diners.

LA CASITA CAFÉ

DESIGN: EL ESTUDIO™ **PHOTOGRAPHY**: MARÍA LAURA BENAVENTE

La Casita Café is a cozy coffee and restaurant space based in Tenerife, the Canary Islands. The brand promotes freshness, comfort, warmth and personality. The restaurant desires to make the experience of their customers unforgettable.
Using hand-drawn illustrations of teapots, cups, saucepans, casseroles and other kitchen equipment, el estudio™ designed a myriad of pattern that became La Casita Café's main visual identity. These motifs were applied throughout the consumer experience to play up the endless, fun options available for diners.

MOLLICA

DESIGN: MARGHERITA MASCIARIELLO

Mollica is a "slow food" brand line, a project-study on sustainable food packaging. The identity message is an invitation to eat organic grown-locally ingredients, valuing and sharing each regional menu of Italian culinary art, to support the development of a more sustainable local food system. A new way to enjoy and taste DOC-guaranteed products in a single cost-effective food retail line. The packaging is designed to be a functional and smart guideline to eat more consciously and healthy: it features the same eco-friendly brand concept by using veggie illustrations, recycled materials, sustainable printings, a natural colour palette. Mollica means "a little piece of", as a little taste to rediscover the time to enjoy the authentic flavor.

LULU CAKE BOUTIQUE

AGENCY: PECK & CO. **CREATIVE DIRECTION/DESIGN:** BENJI PECK

Lulu Cake Boutique, located in New York, crafts masterpieces. Their cakes are unmatched in flavor and artistry. The branding had to retain that same attention to detail, delicate beauty and classic aesthetic, while allowing their tongue-in-cheek personality to show through in unique moments.

ALL DAYS ARE LUCKY CAFÉ

DESIGN: MARYANA SHARENKOVA, KRISTINA SAVINSKAYA

All Days Are Lucky is a small eclectic café located in Saint-Petersburg, Russia. Having its concept "coffee & more", the place serves homemade pasta, basic breakfasts, and desserts. There is no wi-fi in the café in order to encourage live but not virtual communication or working. So take-away option looks reasonable here as well.

The cafe has two equally used names: the long "All days are lucky" and the short "Lucky Days". Elegant and sophisticated logo with a unicorn on it implies discreet corporate identity while the floral print brings a refreshing touch.

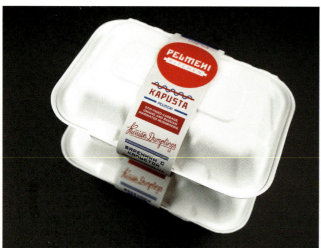

PELMENI KITCHEN

DESIGN: MAGDALENA KSIEZAK

Pelmeni Kitchen is a modern Russian food cart. Specializing in Russian dumplings served hot and available for take-away frozen. The packaging design was created as a cost effective solution to accommodate different flavors and an expanding menu.

JAMIE OLIVER AT GATWICK

AGENCY: THE PLANT

With Jamie's Italian and Union Jacks under its umbrella, Jamie Oliver's presence at Gatwick Airport needed more than just an awkward blend of the two brands.
The Plant created a whole new identity based on the joy of flying and travel and wished the new enterprise Bon Voyage!

AVESSO

DESIGN: ANOIK **PHOTOGRAPHY:** MI MITRIKA, ANOIK

From the beginning, the project's brief has been set upon the combination of three essential elements: three axes in which the logo and consequent graphic identity should rest.

The first was tradition, or the sense of cultural preservation, translated to the engraving (or engraved-looking illustrations) regarding old objects, animals, and some cultural references. The second was personality, or an indie look showing the handmade, personal, and young character of this small local business, translated through the lettering. The third was diversity, a gallery, a restaurant, and a bar combined into a multi-faceted business. Therefore it has an ever-changing logo with more than 30 different illustrations.

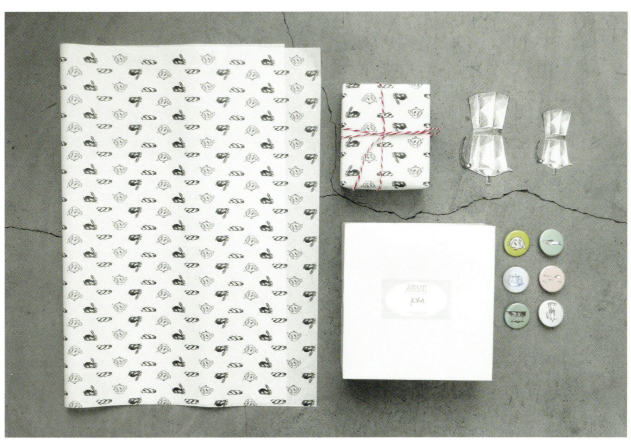

SUI

DESIGN: DANA NOF

A new branding for a sushi restaurant and packaging for the take-away set. All are inspired by the science lab setting. It is Dana Nof's opinion that there is something very clean and precise in the way we eat sushi, which resembles the way a lab researcher works. People hold the sushi in perfect equilibrium using two slim sticks and every person has his own way to add sauces ginger and wasabi. It has to be perfect - not too much nor too little.

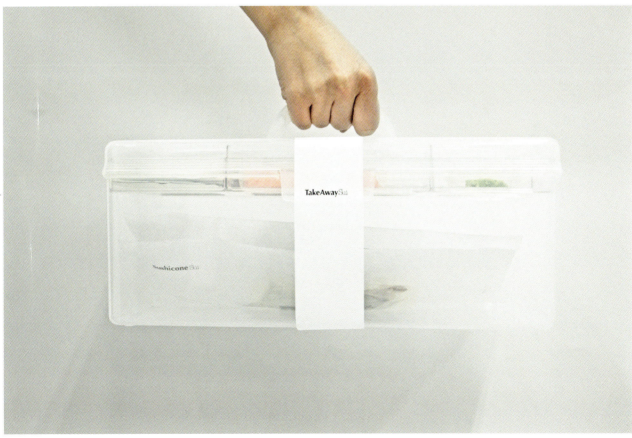

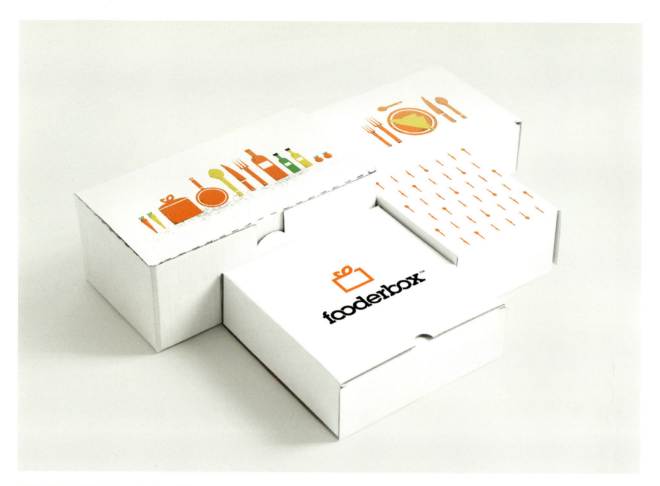

FOODERBOX

AGENCY: KEJJO **CREATIVE DIRECTION/ART DIRECTION:** MICHAL SYCZ **DESIGN:** TOMASZ KWIECIEN

FooderBox is a food boutique where you can order online fresh products and with chef-designed recipe they cook your perfect meal in even less than 30 minutes. There are several ways to order food via service - monthly subscriptions or onetime purchase. Choose the delivery date and enjoy the dish yourself.

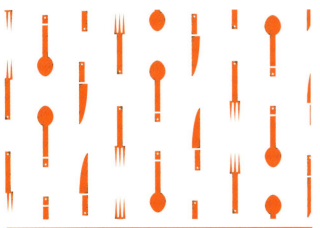

**We deliver
You cook**

BILLION DOLLAR COFFEE

DESIGN: DOOHEE LIM

Doohee Lim's motto is "simple" and he tries to present the beauty of structured letters. He created logo system, pictogram, packaging, all other print collaterals, shop artworks, advertisements, etc. Also he participated in interior design such as choosing wall material, menu and store signage.

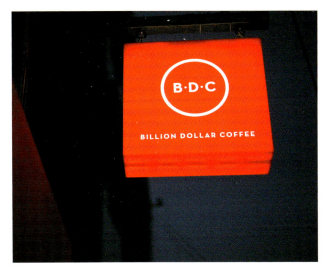

WONDERLUST BAKERY & COFFEE

DESIGN: KUP HUYNH

Wonderlust is a contemporary bakery and coffee shop based in Da Nang city, Viet Nam. The desire is to satisfy your sweet tooth with delectable, homemade bakery items, such as cupcakes, tarts, donuts, specially fresh baked cakes made in their kitchen daily, served with good coffee, drinks and happy people; and by "Wonderlust" they mean, the ambition to perfection from fresh tasting goodness and professional services. The design execution was created from 7 lines of a hexagon which symbolizes perfect balance coming together to form a single-minded entity of the letter "W".

JOE'S COFFEE

AGENCY: REVERT DESIGN **DESIGN:** TREVOR FINNEGAN

Graphic and interior design for new speciality coffee shop based in Dublin's city centre. The design is based around 1950's New York diner with an industrial feel.

WEEKEND

DESIGN: ROANDCO

Weekend is a coffee shop located in the Joule Hotel in downtown Dallas, TX. Spearheaded by the team behind the fashion-forward accessories store TenOverSix, the café has become a relaxing everyday haunt for vacationers to enjoy their coffee. Inspired by Cartoonish film titles from '80s movies like National Lampoon, RoAndCo designed a Weekend logo to convey the bold and cheerful spirit of the brand, balancing that playful youthfulness with a minimal and refined typographic system.

133

PUBLIC DELISHOP

AGENCY: LA TORTILLERÍA

La Tortilleria were given the riveting task of creating the brand identity of a new restaurant at the airport. Inspired by the lively pubs of the UK, they named the place PUBLIC, a deli shop to make a traveler's life easier. Their goal was to create a stylish, yet relaxed place that offered its clients different options to eat whether their flight is delayed, or they're just grabbing a quick bite.

La Tortillería wanted the place to make a difference encouraging people to conspire in favor of an eco friendly environment. So, they decided to have some fun with the meaning of the word "public" and use phrases related to it printed on their easy to recycle and reuse bags, napkins, cups, etc. Airport dining has improved tremendously in the past few years, and it is places like Public that make this possible. Public was a complete success. La Tortilleria took care of everything from their logo and catch phrases to the stationery and packaging materials.

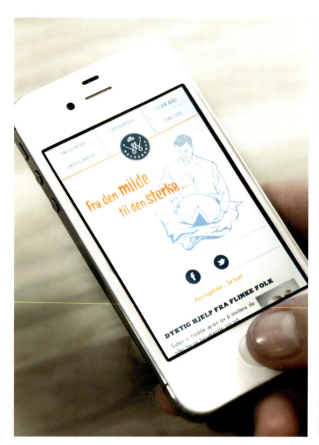

MELKERAMPA

AGENCY: SCANDINAVIAN DESIGN GROUP, INNE DESIGN **PHOTOGRAPHY:** SCANDINAVIAN DESIGN GROUP, MONA GUNDERSEN

At Melkerampa, TINE's new brandstore at Oslo's food-hall, the traditional meets the modern in a symbiosis of visual identity and interior design. The interior of the Melkerampa store allows for both selling and serving and it's fleshed out through the use of elements from the visual identity. The long table acts as the centerpiece to the store, inviting visitors to rest a while and maybe chat with their tablemates. In developing the identity the designers focused on the long dairy culture which TINE has been a major part of over the last 130 years, and gave them a modern expression. The name Melkerampa conjures up images of the rich tradition of a social meeting place.

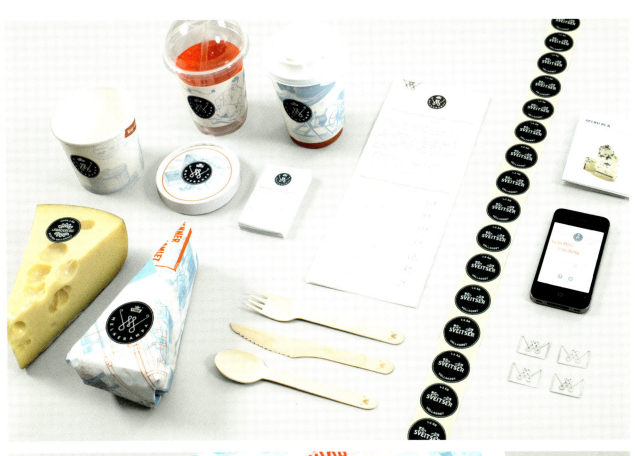

TART BLANC

DESIGN: MANIC DESIGN

Tart Blanc is an artisanal bakery in Singapore specialising in beautiful tarts featuring inventive flavour and texture combinations. The owners, a pair of sisters, one of whom is the baker, tell Manic Design that they dream of multi-layered tarts exploding with flavours and textures. To underline the "tartistry" of the baked goods, they came up with the name "tart blanc" which is inspired by "carte blanche", which means blank paper and expresses the idea that anything is possible. For the packaging and namecards, they chose an unusual and raw grey substrate as an alternative to the ubiquitous kraft to hint at the human-made, small batch nature of the bakery. It took them a very long time to convince the box maker to make the boxes in this material but they think that the results are worth every minute trying to get it right.

THE WHITE LINE

DESIGN: DANA NOF

With the Israeli economic and social reality in the background, Dana Nof was requested to design economic packaging for several basic goods. From her point of view, economic packaging doesn't necessarily mean over sizes packaging which addresses a certain type of consumer and ignores bachelors and young couples who cannot enjoy the benefits of such packaging.
With that in mind she designed a packaging line with an emphasis on multi-packaging. This allows for smaller "personal" portions to be kept fresh for long periods of time. This packaging line includes: bread, eggs, sugar, rice and bleach.

JAIME BERIESTAIN CONCEPT STORE

DESIGN/PHOTOGRAPHY: MATHIAS MARTIN

The well-known interior designer Jaime Beriestain opens his own social place in Barcelona. It's 500 square meters with a shop and a restaurant. For the packaging, Mathias Martin chose a geometric shape in order to develop it differently: the shop (very colorful, modern and energetic), restaurant (black and white as the traditional parisian bistrot) and handmade for the handmade products gourmet.

THE BREADLINE EATERY (ISTD BRIEF 2013)

GRAPHIC DESIGN/ART DIRECTION: RENE HERMAN

Everything on the menu costs $1.25 or less to make. 1,345 million people live below the extreme poverty line (also known as the "breadline"), which is $1.25. Consumers pay double the cost price for a meal and the difference goes to providing necessary food for those living under the breadline. By enjoying a simple meal, consumers are able to identify with the plight of the poor and contribute to their lives at the same time.

SHOREDITCH GRIND CAFE

DESIGN/ILLUSTRATION: SEAN GALLAGHER

Shoreditch Grind is an amalgamation combining a boutique cafe and recording studio set within a unique oval building on a busy roundabout in Shoreditch, London. The theme for the cafe was to be bold and new while retaining an authentic nature.

SALVATION JANE CAFE

DESIGN/ILLUSTRATION: SEAN GALLAGHER

Salvation Jane Cafe is the sister store to Lantana Cafe so it had the same theme and identity as the original cafe but had to be updated to appeal to a new demographic as it was opened in Shoreditch, London.

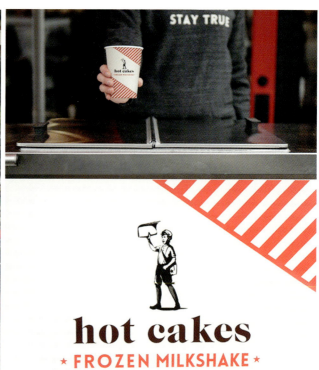

HOT CAKES MOLTEN CHOCOLATE CAKERY

DESIGN: CREATIVE RETAIL PACKAGING, INC.(CRP)

Hot Cakes Molten Chocolate Cakery located in Seattle, WA crafts organic, classic American comfort desserts and innovative confections. Founded in 2008 by Autumn Martin, the restaurant is named after its signature product: "take 'n bake" molten chocolate cakes. CRP helped to create a cohesive brand impression through product packaging, marketing collateral, and storefront design. Utilizing a consistent "sash" element inspired by the newsboy's messenger bag, each product line is differentiated by unique patterns and a rich color palette to harmoniously convey an earthy, yet high-end aesthetic.

LA MAGIA (THE MAGIC)

DESIGN: FERNANDA GODOY

Identity proposal for a coffee shop brand called La Magia (The Magic). This project was inspired by the magical atmosphere of an apothecary.

BLUE PEACH

ART DIRECTION/DESIGN: KONSTANTINA YIANNAKOPOULOU ILLUSTRATION: YVONNE IOSIFELLI

Blue Peach is a Coffee-Music bar that remains one of the oldest haunts of Athens and is more than just a neighborhood café-bar. Small, warm, cozy, with ambient lighting, elements of wood and mostly DIY decoration, were the main things that guided the new identity. Customized illustrations and logo design, inspired mainly by the 60's, strengthen the old-style, not in outdated way. The applications, such as the take-away packagings, were designed in order to keep the strong character of the store as well as the outside, to attract the eyes of passers-by.

DAVAJ DELIKATESSEN

AGENCY: PLANET CREATIVE **ART DIRECTION/DESIGN:** THOMAS ANDERSSON, TOBIAS OTTOMAR

Davaj Delikatessen concept is a homage to the deli's of Little Odessa, New York. Offering sandwiches and beverage with the taste of eastern Europe, Davaj Deli is the opposite to the rustic decorated and generic bakery's/coffee shops in Sweden. Maybe because it's the only one where you can have a shot of vodka together with your bagel.

First of all Planet Creative created a "factory" logo. This "factory" logo would be the sender of all the prints, signage and deli products. Each and everyone produced on different kind of materials. This would also be the complement to the main logo. After that they also created logotypes for the sandwiches, with different styles for each, that would also work as sub brands with their own history and place.

KOIKI

AGENCY: BROWN FOX STUDIO **CREATIVE DIRECTION:** FERGIE TAN **DESIGN:** AMELIA AGUSTINE

KOIKI is a Japanese eatery that focuses on everyday dishes, with a modern touch. With this in mind, Brown Fox Studio's task was to develop a brand with a casual tone, but also contemporary.

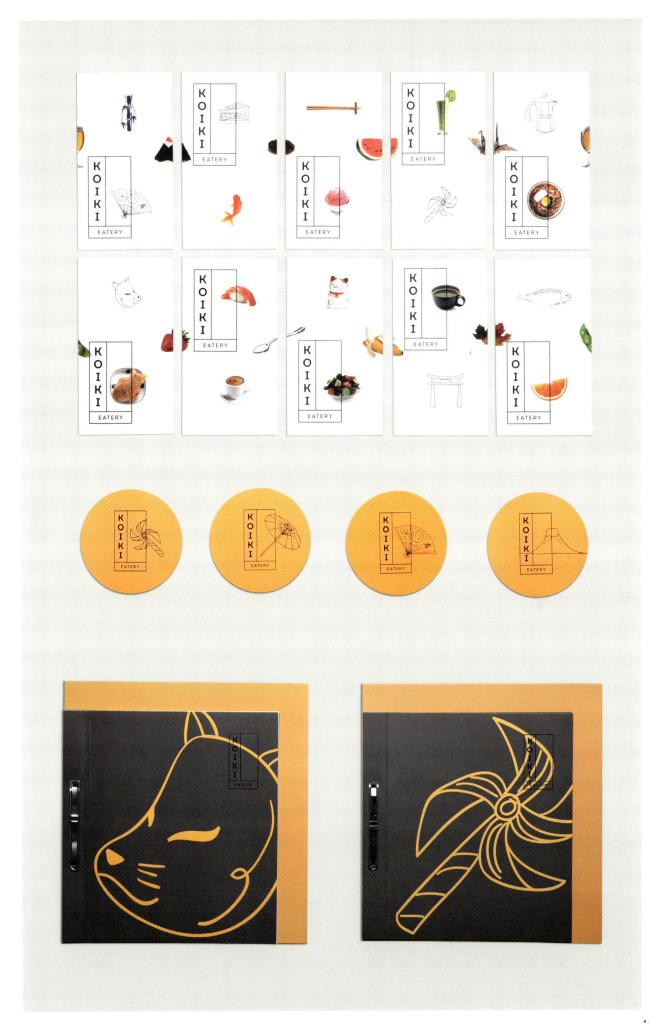

1 BITE 2 GO CAFÉ & DELI

AGENCY: ACCENT COLLECTIVE **DESIGN:** DENNIS CHANG, JEAN LEE **ILLUSTRATION:** REACH

1 Bite 2 Go is an American diner serving a variety of classic sandwiches that will satisfy one's delicatessen craving. Accent participated in shaping the brand from naming to visual identity design, as well as interior decoration. The name "1 Bite 2 Go" intends to promote a healthy, energetic and fulfilling lifestyle, encouraging people to eat well and be active in life. Guests may enjoy the delicious bites for here or for to go. The generous portions and mouth-watering taste will make anyone take one extra bite.

OTHER COFFEE®

AGENCY: EMPATÍA®

There's nothing better than the aroma of freshly brewed coffee. other coffee® is committed to being a great place for people who love coffee and harmonious places. With simple treats this newly coffee bar offers high quality coffee products. Looking for a simple yet stylish brand, they approach Empatía® to create their whole image. They designed a strong, seductive and elegant brand down to the last detail, including packaging and stationery. Where lie the roots of this brand? A simple expression of a simple business idea.

CAFFÈ FRUTTA

DESIGN: WAN LING SU

The brand name originates from Italian, Caffè Frutta means coffee beans. "沐果" means immersing in the scent of coffee. The hand-drawn designed logo presents heartwarmingness and friendliness. Also the picture is composed mainly of coffee beans, like raindrop, to present the smell of coffee around you like warm rain.

The word type is slender and simple. The logo's standard colors are black, white, and grey. It can be used around or combined with several images.

LE BOUQUET BREAD & BAKERY

AGENCY: ACCENT COLLECTIVE **DESIGN:** DENNIS CHANG, JEAN LEE

Le bouquet Bread & Bakery is an authentic French bakery shop located in Taipei city. Accent employs a simple color palette of yellow and toasted brown that depicts the tastiness of well-baked breads. The clean packaging with vintage French posters and homeware decoration, creates a fresh and amicable brand identity.

LES BÉBÉS CUPCAKERY

AGENCY: ACCENT COLLECTIVE **DESIGN:** JEAN LEE

Les Bébés Cupcakery, the first cupcake speciality shop in Taiwan featuring mini size cupcakes, approached Accent to help create a joyous yet elegant brand image. Accent designed a clean rhythmic logotype reflecting the simplicity and elegance of the cupcakes. Inspired by frostings on the cupcakes, Accent then developed numerous patterns wonderful for packaging and interior decor. The different combinations of packaging and a wide assortment of cupcake flavors makes any visit constantly fun and encourages people to share joy and laughter with loved ones.

ELIZABETH STREET CAFÉ

AGENCY: FÖDA STUDIO **CREATIVE DIRECTION:** JETT BUTLER **DESIGN:** EMILY SAWTELLE, JETT BUTLER

Noodles, báhn mi, boulangerie. Elizabeth Street Cafe comes to South First street. Elizabeth Street Cafe marries French, Vietnamese and Austin food culture. The brand identity addresses every detail as a family of graphic components, as opposed to a logo to be replicated. The identity does double duty supporting the brand as a boulangerie in the morning and transforming to a noodle house in the afternoon and evening. The heavy use of pattern fields and blended typefaces suggest the number of ingredients to be found in the dishes. Subtle acts of subversion can be found, like placing French iconography in places usually reserved for Asian art references. In one single mark Elizabeth Street Cafe is both quaint and international, candy like but structured, nostalgic yet fresh. Bon appétit!

DOS CINCUENTA & CINCO FOODTRUCK

DESIGN: ANA LUCÍA MONTES, NATALIA MÉNDEZ, LUISA ARAGÓN, MONTSERRAT CHÁVEZ

Dos Cincuenta & Cinco Foodtruck is the result of a graphic design thesis project in the University of Monterrey. The challenge was to find a graphic solution to a food truck that wants to introduce itself to the Mexican gastronomic market, having a special focus on young adults between 18 and 35 years old. It has a 50's fair vibe, where the food truck will be the place where the consumer can experience a different kind of culinary involvement. From being served by fair-like character to finding your own fortune in your takeaway box. The customers will approve, remember and share their new experience, creating a very close relationship between the restaurant and its customers.

RITARU COFFEE

DESIGN: COMMUNE **PHOTOGRAPHY**: KEI FURUSE

Ritaru Coffee is a roaster and cafe in Sapporo. They make a great deal of "time" to roast coffee beans, serve coffee, choose a cup, and provide a time to have coffee and rest at Ritaru Coffee. Commune found inspiration for the visual identity from a tree stump as symbol of "time".

SAMSUNG CLUB DES CHEFS

AGENCY: EXTRÊME CORPORATE **CREATIVE DIRECTION**: ROMAIN ROGER **ART DIRECTION**: ROMAIN ROGER, FLORENTIN BERNARD, SÉBASTIEN KOPIOWSKI **DESIGN**: CATHERINE KURAL

Simplicity, modernity and elegance are the signature of this new club created by Samsung. Showcasing the know-how and the experience of Michelin's star-rated chefs and food visionaries around the world, Samsung's Club des Chefs brings some of the freshest inspirations and ideas to help everyone rediscover the pleasures of cooking fresh and healthy food. The name selected is actually a way to incarnate the prestige of French cuisine and the country's rich food culture. Using new gastronomic cuisine codes where technology innovation meets premium design, the identity of this Club wishes to concentrate on what is essential: the chef's expertise and professionalism.

22.13 FAVORITE PLACE

AGENCY: GLOBALPOINT AGENCY RUSSIA SAINT-PETERSBURG **ART DIRECTION**: SEREBRENNIKOV RODION **GRAPHIC DESIGN**: SEREBRENNIKOV RODION, DIANA SERGIENKO

22.13 is a two-storied restaurant and bar in the heart of St.Petersburg. Inspired by the favorite places around the world the owners have created a unique place in eclectic style, with cosmopolitan cuisine, delightful confectionery and own library.

MAMALU

DESIGN: KIDSTUDIO **PHOTOGRAPHY:** STEFANO CASATI

Our taste is what makes us who we are. It makes our houses warmer, our loved ones lovelier and our food yummier. Mamalu - done with taste.

"XIAO XIAO SE HUI" URBAN BAKERY

AGENCY: ALLCAN DESIGN **DESIGN:** LILY CHAN

"Xiao Xiao Se Hui" is a bakery located in urban corner. When the brand was just founded, Allcan Design hopes to convey the simple, unadorned and freewheeling feelings, and at the same time, have a little personality and disposition. For example, the symbol overall follows traditional seal form and blends simple bow tie figures. The doggy bags do not need to be printed. We only need to affix two seals on them before use. The decoration in the shop uses a lot of old woods. The metal doorknob, which is carved with the brand symbol, oxidized naturally. The backstage kitchen and the antechamber are separated by transparent glass, so guests can see the making of bread and cakes clearly.

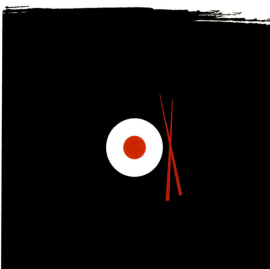

JIMO

AGENCY: SMART! GRUPO CREATIVO

Jimo is a food delivery store dedicated to Asian food, which allowed the agency to address a project in a gastronomic sector without a referent in Mar del Plata.

Using a simple image that optimizes a chromatic aspect, a system easy to implement and reproduce, effectively maintaining the authenticity and personalty was created to add value to the brand which was essential for the company's growth.

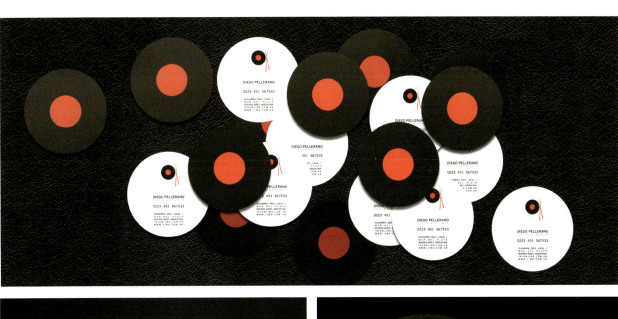

TRANSIT RESTAURANT

AGENCY: STUDIO HAUSHERR

With the rather bold and simple design, Studio Hausherr wanted to emphasize the fast and quick culture in the metropolitan neighborhood surrounding the restaurant. Transit Restaurant functions successfully as a starting point for a young crowd before hopping to the surrounding bars and clubs. So it truly is a transit restaurant.

PIZZA VINOTECA

AGENCY: MEMO, NYC. **CREATIVE DIRECTION:** DOUGLAS RICCARDI

The founder of Pizza Vinoteca wanted to create a fast-casual restaurant and take-out destination that would redefine casual dining in New York. The goal was to create a highly designed experience where the best of fine dining was available at a great price in a technology-enhanced environment. For the takeout packaging, Memo wanted guests to leave with a tailored, high style package which looked more like it came from a high-end boutique than from a fast casual restaurant. This reinforces the restaurant's mission of delivering an elevated experience at a value price.

THE SANDWICH SHOP

THE SANDWICH SHOP

THE SANDWICH SHOP

LIFE IS LIKE A SANDWICH YOU HAVE TO FILL IT WITH THE BEST INGREDIENTS

PEACE + LOAF

THE SANDWICH SHOP

DESIGN: PHIL ROBSON

Brand creation for a Sydney based sandwich shop. Keeping things simple, clean and concise. A nod to the past, with a sophisticated graphic design language and palette.

TOCK'S

AGENCY: POLYGRAPHE **DESIGN:** DAVID KESSOUS, SÉBASTIEN BISSON **ACCOUNT DIRECTOR:** MARIE-CLAUDE FORTIN **ILLUSTRATION:** DAVID KESSOUS, SÉBASTIEN BISSON

After a lot of thoughts, negotiations and trips to China, Richard Tock, a well known successful Montreal's businessman, decided to open the first real smoked meat restaurant in Shanghai. Studio Polygraphe's mandate was to elaborate the complete brand identity. From the name, logo, restaurant's interior decoration, uniforms, table-mats, menu, glasses, take out bags to signage.

Their strategy was to export the Montreal's smoked meat tradition to China in a very homy, welcoming, easy going way. As a homage to the smoked meat deli's traditions and its founder, but also to give a unique and personal touch to the brand, they decided to hand-write every piece of graphic elements and typographic detail. The results are above expectations. The restaurant is a success. A franchise is now born and two new Tock's are on the way.

SUNRISE BAKERY
DESIGN/ILLUSTRATION: EKTA PATEL

Sunrise Bakery is a new bakery located in west Auckland, New Zealand.

THE WINEY COW

DESIGN: CHARLOTTE FOSDIKE

The Winey Cow had their own range of cheeses and wines that their customers could purchase. Charlotte Fosdike designed the packages for them, as well as the unique menu.

THE FOOD BOX

DESIGN: ROD CASTRO **PHOTOGRAPHY:** JORGE MALO, DANIEL ARRONIZ

The Food Box is a restaurant with a unique made from scratch quality taste that has the best burgers in the city of Monterrey. It initially started as a fast-food delivery service and now works both as a delivery and burger boutique restaurant due to its success and demand.
The graphic concept was to create a minimal yet functional modern design with pattern shapes that reflected the brand's bold and unique culinary process.

Food Delivery Boutique · Plaza Tanazco · T - 81112691

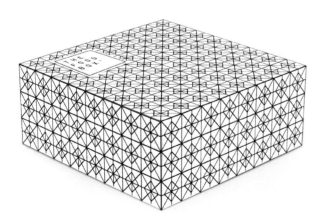

THE RITTENHOUSE KITCHEN

DESIGN: BONNIE SILVERBERG

Brand concept for a restaurant located in Philadelphia, PA, whose tagline is, "Worldly Cuisine Locally Grown."

SUSY'S BAKERY

AGENCY: PARA TODO HAY FANS ® **ART DIRECTION/DESIGN:** MOISÉS E. GUILLÉN ROMERO **DESIGN DIRECTION:** GUILLERMO CASTELLANOS FLORES
PHOTOGRAPHY: JANI ELIZABETH RANGEL LUCERO

Susy's Bakery ® is a premium quality bakery and food retail space founded and established by Azucena Romero Camarena since 1976 in Guadalajara, Mexico. The corporate identity is directly derived from the profile of the company: a small business which bakes signature gourmet cookies, cakes, cupcakes, pies, and choux, priding itself of having the best homemade touch of the region. Susy's Bakery's packaging is quite simple and very easy to apply; Para Todo Hay Fans ® use parchment paper to wrap different products, which is printed with a pattern of pictograms specially designed for the brand. Circular stickers are also printed with pictograms to stick on laminated packaging; finally, they use recycled paper bags printed with different designs, each made for small bags and for larger bags.

TUCKER & BEVVY

AGENCY: WALL-TO-WALL STUDIOS **DESIGN:** SCOTT NAAUAO

Branding proposal for Tucker & Bevvy, a picnic food store featuring Sydney-inspired cuisine. The store, located across the street from the beaches of Waikiki, gets its name from the Australian slang of "Food & Drink" and focuses around the idea of "feeding the beach" by offering fresh juice, smoothies, sandwiches and salads.

For this concept, Scott Naauao was inspired by a Hobo-Dyer Map he came across on the internet that had the hemispheres - flipped around. He played up the idea of food coming "from Down Under" by creating a brand that had elements intentionally upside down to create a juxtaposition between Hawaii and Australia.

PUNCHCARD

PURCHASE 7 SANDWICHES OR
SALADS AND GET THE 8TH FREE

TUCKER & BEVVY

PUNCHCARD

PURCHASE 7 SANDWICHES OR
SALADS AND GET THE 8TH FREE

TUCKER & BEVVY

L'ÉCLAIR

DESIGN AGENCY: STUDIO WABA **DESIGN:** JOANA ROCHA & PEDRO MOTTA

L'Éclair is a French patisserie that opened in Lisboa, Portugal, in May 2014. This new concept focused mainly on éclairs. Studio WABA were asked to join the project by the architecture team SD JM Arq, who needed help with the wall decoration, but they also ended up developing all the brand communication, packaging included, since the patisserie only had the logo (by Devil Design Deluxe).

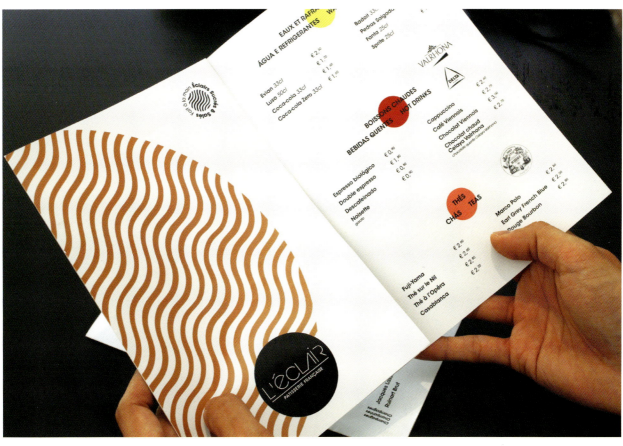

THIS IS ONE
ESPECIALLY
fabulous
— HOT CHOCOLATE —

THIS
Chai Latte
IS SERIOUSLY
SPICEY

THIS COFFEE
HAS BEEN
So good to me!

PAPER CUP

DESIGN: CHARLOTTE FOSDIKE

Paper Cup was a bold and exciting project. The client was after an edgy and colourful style for their brand. They were also looking for a coffee cup design that would be something their customers want to use again. With the use of bright colours, simple patterns and fun typography, Charlotte Fosdike was able to create a brand that would speak the values of their business.

LA CAMPANA

AGENCY: COMITÉ STUDIO   **ART DIRECTION/DESIGN:** IBON APEZTEGUIA, FRANCESC MORATA

La Campana has been producing handmade nougat bars and ices since 1980. To redesign the ice cream parlour next to their famous shop in Barcelona, the designers created a logo inspired by the modernist, and a print that takes a wink at the nearby Picasso museum.

LA CAMPANA

100% natural

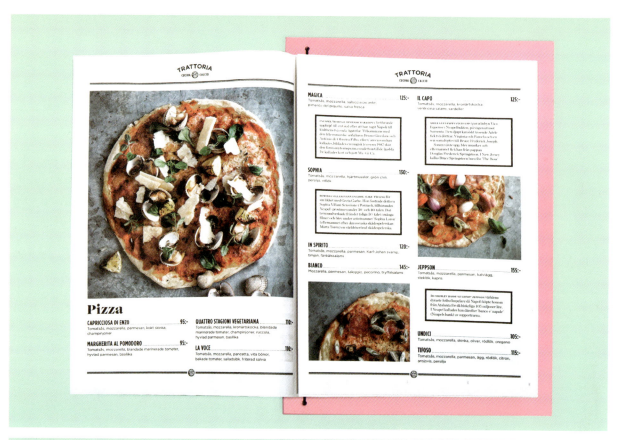

ENZO'S

AGENCY: PLANET CREATIVE **ART DIRECTION/DESIGN:** THOMAS ANDERSSON, TOBIAS OTTOMAR

Enzo's is an Italian trattoria and sports bar: a rustic eatery, where a relaxed atmosphere and simple, good food are significant. Here you can enjoy Neapolitan food and watch the latest league games in Italian football.

Inspired by the Neapolitan spirit and the Swedish football legends who played there, Planet Creative created the whole brand with heritage both from Sweden and Italy.

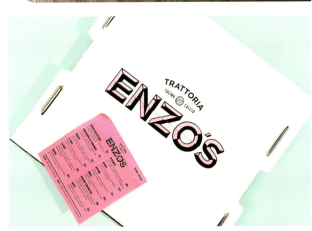

GELATO MIO

AGENCY: SQUAD INK **DESIGN:** MATTHEW SQUADRITO, TERRY SQUADRITO

Gelato Mio is an artisan gelateria in Queensland, Australia. This hidden gem crafts authentic Italian gelato using traditional techniques and only the best local produce. From the get-go Squad Ink wanted the concept to be playful and appeal to all ages. The slight retro style graphics and use of typography play to the artisan nature of the product and a more mature audience. The playful gelato air balloon illustration acts as the mascot of the brand, and brings to life a child like fantasy.

EAT

AGENCY: THE PLANT

EAT creates great food-to-go with an attention to detail and curiosity that's unique in their sector. Staffed by a team of committed foodies their menu is a constantly changing offer of old favourites and new treats.
Every ingredient and recipe is carefully chosen and it's this sentiment of "handcrafted" that defines the essence of the EAT brand.

213

FRAE FROZEN YOGURT

AGENCY: THE PLANT

All sourced from a single farm in Wales, Frae Frozen Yogurt was a step ahead in terms of its product.
The Plant's task was to turn a great product into a great brand. They have given Frae a voice, injecting fun, humour and confidence into the brand. They have built a flexible system that allows the brand to grow and express itself in different ways. From a typography system based on vintage dairy graphics to beautiful, natural and intimate photography. The Frae brand has everything in place to become an international brand.

GLACE ARTISAN ICE CREAM

AGENCY: STIR AND ENJOY **CREATIVE DIRECTION/COPYWRITING:** BRENT ANDERSON **DESIGN:** NATHANIEL COOPER

Kansas City-based Glace (say it this way, "Gla-say") Artisan Ice Cream is a more grown-up sweet treat expression, rich in texture and inventive flavors like Venezuelan dark chocolate, fleur de sel caramel and pineapple-cilantro sorbet. The corresponding brand expression is clean, sophisticated and a nod to the owner's love of modern minimalism.

At the same time, the copy and color palette make the brand feel fun and approachable. The logo also incorporates a sly tie to ice cream with circles that look like melting "drips" hitting the floor, while tailored graphic elements help the identity look fashionable and unexpected in the category.

HORNHUSET

AGENCY: PLANET CREATIVE **ART DIRECTION/DESIGN:** THOMAS ANDERSSON, TOBIAS OTTOMAR

Hornhuset is like a bustling little square somewhere around the Mediterranean. A melting pot on three floors for those who want to enjoy a menu of flavourful, smaller dishes, or buy exceptionally tasty take out.

Hornhuset is a mix of all the good things from around the Mediterranean and that is something the designers wanted to get through in the identity. Fresh bold colours, a playful typography and frame to bind it together. All with a sun bleached feeling of summer.

COMAXURROS

DESIGN: LO SIENTO **ILLUSTRATION:** BROSMIND

Comaxurros is a new concept of xurreria. A "churro", sometimes referred to as a Spanish donut, is a fried-dough pastry, predominantly choux-based snack.

COMAXuRROS°

The fried community

C/ Muntaner, 562
Barcelona 08022
+34 93 417 94 05
info@comaxurros.com
www.comaxurros.com

BOCHOCO

DESIGN: MARINA GOÑI **PHOTOGRAPHY:** OLGA RUÍZ **RETAIL:** SUA INTERIORISMO

Naming and identity for a new concept of signature cake shop. The name bochoco borns from the union of "botxo", popular name for Bilbao and choco (chocolate).
The identity had to be away from the classic image of traditional cake shop to emphasize values such as minimalism, purity and modernity.

COZMO CAFE

AGENCY: WONDEREIGHT **CREATIVE DIRECTION:** WALID NASRALA, KARIM ABOURIZK **ART DIRECTION/DESIGN/PHOTOGRAPHY:** KARIM ABOURIZK

The brief was a concept offering a wide range of start food offering. WonderEight were commissioned to create a brand that offers a casual-chic experience. And as the restaurant was opening in the most prestigious Yachting club in Beirut, they set the challenge of creating a balance between a casual, chic and maritime feel.

TAVERNA BRILLO

AGENCY: PLANET CREATIVE **ART DIRECTION/DESIGN:** THOMAS ANDERSSON, TOBIAS OTTOMAR

The owners of high-end restaurants Sturehof, Riche and Teatergrillen have opened their fourth and largest restaurant so far, inspired by the Italian kitchen. As with the other restaurants in the group, the dining area is surrounded by bars and will furthermore also encompass a market, a bakery, a greenhouse and an ice-cream café.

Planet Creative applied and developed the logotype created by the Swedish designer Monica Eskedahl for the visual identity, on everything from menu and take away products to the website.

TRIED & TRUE

DESIGN: BAGS OF JOY

Tried & True is an independent cafè in Putney, London. Bags of Joy created a new brand language and developed a new interior tone of voice that suited brand. They worked hand in hand with founder Rob Kelly to deliver the final experience. Drop by for a coffee and check it out!

SECRET LOCATION

DESIGN: SABOTAGEPKG PHOTOGRAPHY: STUDIO21

SabotagePKG have designed the entire packaging range for Secret Location concept store Vancouver, Canada.
Capturing the essence of the Vancouver concept store's unique brand, and applying it to each facet of the customer experience for both retail and food.
Taking the store's existing brand and ethos of originality, quality and craftsmanship, SabotagePKG created bespoke designs to complement the unique in-store experience – from the desirable, uniquely designed carrier bag right down to the small, sublime coffee cups & bespoke carrier for the store's tasting room.

SANOMA CAFÉ

AGENCY: KUUDES KERROS **ART DIRECTION/DESIGN**: TONY ERAPURO **COPYWRITING**: MIKKO MAKINEN **ARCHITECT**: JANNE KUPIAINEN
STRATEGY DIRECTION: JARI DANIELSSON **PHOTOGRAPHY**: PAAVO LEHTONEN

The leading Finnish multi-channel media company, Sanoma Media Finland, livened up their impressive corporate glass building with a new ground floor café. The nature of an ever-changing media was used as a foundation for the café's visual communication, which is comprised of graphical elements – pixels and speech bubbles – that represent an interactive media that is constantly present. The new visual identity was then extended into different elements ranging from paper cups to napkins. Now the different voices of customers, passersby, schoolchildren, metropolitan mums and Sanoma Media Finland are all united in collective speech bubbles.

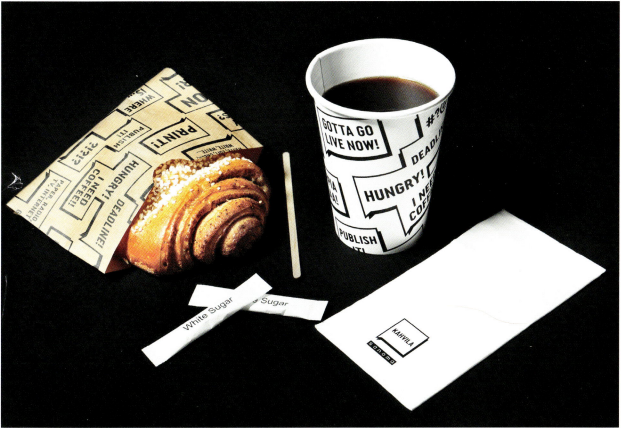

INDEX

Foreign Policy Design Group

p.028-029, 048-049
Foreign Policy Design Group is a team of idea makers & story tellers who help clients and brands realize and evolve their brands with creative and strategic deployment of traditional terrestrial channel & digital media channels. Helmed by Creative Directors Yah-Leng Yu and Arthur Chin, the group works on a good smorgasbord of projects ranging from creative/art direction and design, branding, brand strategy, digital strategy, strategic research and marketing campaign services for luxury fashion and lifestyle brands, fast-moving consumer goods brands, arts and cultural institution as well as think tank consultancies.

www.foreignpolicydesign.com

FROM GRAPHIC

p.066-067
FROM GRAPHIC is a graphic design company in Tokyo, founded by Yoko Maruyama in 2009. "Colors", "Shapes", and "Materials". Finding a perfect one from their infinite combinations is FROM GRAPHIC's job.

www.fromgraphic.jp

G

Garbergs Project

p.040-041, 070-071
Garbergs Project is a design and concept agency, driven by ideas with long experience of brand development. With creativity, strategy, curiosity and craftsmanship they create long lasting brands for their customers.

Garbergs Project offer customers their expertise throughout the design process: Brand strategy, visual identities, packaging design, concept design, naming, book design, etc.

www.garbergsproject.se

GLOBALPOINT Agency Russia Saint-Petersburg

p.178-179
GLOBALPOINT Agency Russia Saint-Petersburg is a part of GLOBALPOINTFAMILY Marketing and Advertising Group, an independent business entity that provides a wide range of services within integrated Marcom. Following are the MAG components: Communications Agency Global Point located in St. Petersburg, Moscow and New York; Event Agency Global Point Entertainment; TOP TEAM (trade and consumer promotion); DANCE PLANET (promotion company), GPF Hospitality (design concept and restaurant Franchising team).

www.globalpointagency.com

I

Irina Shirokova

p.102-103
Irina Shirokova is a Russian graphic designer based in Saint-Petersburg. She loves typography, lettering, package design and illustration.

www.be.net/Shuga

J

John Wegman

p.026-027
John is an independent graphic designer from Melbourne, Australia. He works across various mediums with an array of clients. John is also the co-founder of Fifty North, a co-working studio for creatives.

www.johnwegman.com.au

Jorge Atrespuntos

p.094-095
Born on a hot July day in 1989, Jorge is a young graphic designer, graduated from Soria School of Arts and Design in 2013. In mid-2010 he decided to launch the personal project Atrespuntos, name under which he develops projects for entrepreneurs and multidisciplinary companies. He believes in graphic design as an essential communicative tool, facing every design problem as a unique experience, with the idea of communicating a clear and precise message using. Minimal and reductive design is an attribute common throughout most of his work. Jorge is currently a designer at Bisgràfic, a graphic design studio based in Barcelona, and facing other collaborations or personal projects by their own.

www.be.net/jorge-atrespuntos

Jungmin Kim

p.104-105
Jungmin Kim was born in Seoul, Korea in 1986. In her twenties, she studied General Business in Singapore, and then moved to Melbourne, Australia for BA of Communication Design (RMIT University). She has the greatest passion for branding and marketing and is gaining such wonderful learning opportunities in the professional field before she moves onto further studies.

byjungmin.com

K

Kejjo

p.124-125
Formed in 2010, Kejjo is a creative agency with over 8 years of collective experience working closely with local, national and international clients. Kejjo's aim is to create a coherent, original and distinctive design solution that communicates clients' key messages.

www.kejjo.com

KentLyons

p.050-051
KentLyons was formed in 2003 to help brands communicate with people. They produce communications, products and brands that are beautiful and useful — that engage peoples' emotions and work intuitively and effortlessly. They are a hugely talented multidisciplinary team of designers, developers, writers, photographers, illustrators, art directors and creatives.

www.kentlyons.com

Kidstudio

p.180-181
Kidstudio is a design studio in Florence, Italy. Fostered in an environment rich in arts and crafts, history and culture, it is now a leading light in the crowded world of graphics and creativity.

kidstudio.it

Kilo

p.046-047
Kilo is a company that combines design and technology to create experiences in the digital space.

Founded in 2005, Kilo believes that art and technology are seamless and part of the creative process when designing for the web. Over the years, Kilo has collaborated with advertising agencies, design studios and internet startups to clearly define their digital experiences.

The team's area of speciality also covers motion graphics, videos and interactive touch applications.

kilo.sg

Kinetic Singapore

p.106-107
Kinetic is a creative agency based in Singapore.

kinetic.com.sg

Konstantina Yiannakopoulou

p.154-155
Konstantina Yiannakopoulou is a graphic designer, based in Athens, Greece. Restless explorer of the visual world, believer of the functionality and simplicity, devoted to serve communicative solutions providing contemporary, custom, representative and timeless results. Currently Konstantina is Co-founder of the Birthdays Design studio.

www.behance.net/yiannakopoulou

Korn Design

p.084-085
Korn Design is an award-winning brand design and strategy firm based in Boston and New York City. With imagination and intelligence, Korn Design helps businesses craft indelible images that shape perception and impact brand experience. Korn consistently produces work that manages to be simultaneously imaginative and intelligent, refined and rooted. Motivated by the belief that its clients' success is their own, Korn provides expert consultation on diverse assignments in the hospitality, restaurant, luxury-goods, and cultural categories for top-of-class developers, entrepreneurs, chefs, and institutional leaders.

www.korndesign.com

Kup Huynh

p.128-129
Kup Huynh is a freelance graphic designer working in Viet Nam and Singapore. He focuses on branding, print design and photography.

www.behance.net/kuphuynh

Kuudes Kerros

p.230-232
Kuudes Kerros is a design agency in Helsinki, Finland.

www.kuudes.fi

L

La Tortillería

Originally founded in an old tortilla factory building, La Tortillería is a creative company with a passion for images and words with the exceptional ability of turning them into an exquisite reflection of an idea. They create, brand, design, publish and advertise blending creativity and functionality to grant each project a unique personality. They are creative problem solvers who begin with the end in mind either from scratch or from an outlined plan and make things happen come hell or high water.

latortilleria.com

Lo Siento

Lo Siento is specially interested in taking over identity projects as a whole. The main feature of its work is its physical and material approach to the graphic solutions, resulting in a field where graphic and industrial go hand by hand, in a constant search for an alliance with the artisan processes. The paper as an important medium to convey the idea of a warm communication.

www.losiento.net

Louise Skafte

Louise Skafte is an art director from Copenhagen, Denmark. Inspired by her love of food and design she has shaped her style to represent her Scandinavian heritage. That's easily recognized by its minimalistic style, organic shapes and limited colour palette.

With a fine respect for good materials she takes inspirations from both modern design and traditional values.

Currently doing her bachelor in visual communication at DMJX, Louise has worked on several food branding projects that have helped shape her style and enhance her work. Branding for Louise isn't just about identifying a product but creating an experience around it and enhancing the emotional attachment between the consumer and the brand.

cargocollective.com/Louiseskafte

M

Magdalena Ksiezak

Magdalena Ksiezak is a graphic designer and creative based in Melbourne, Australia.

www.hellomagda.com

Mak Yu Jing

Mak Yu Jing is a graphic designer from Singapore. She's recently graduated with a Diploma in Visual Communication at Temasek Polytechnic, School of Design, Singapore.

She enjoys being a versatile communicator and loves the creative and thinking process behind the creation of each project.

Apart from design, Yu Jing loves eating, the smell of carbon paper, music, travelling, film photography, mockumentaries, and other stuff.

www.makyujing.com

Manic Design

Manic Design is an award-winning creative agency with a portfolio of work that ranges from websites and online campaigns to advertising and branding. The studio was founded in 1999 with the belief that good design always includes both creativity and communication. A piece of work that looks great but fails to speak to its audience is not good design. Manic Design have embraced this and cemented it into their culture and their work.

www.wearemanic.com

Margarida Mouta

David Santos, Joana Santos, José Araújo, Margarida Mouta and Maria Branco had graduated in Design at Aveiro University in 2011.

www.behance.net/margaridamouta

Margherita Masciariello

Margherita Masciariello was born in Naples, Italy, in 1983. She's a freelance multidisciplinary designer. After studying Physics at University, she graduated from ILAS Institute of Design in Naples, specializing in Editorial Design and Digital Publishing. Passionate about fashion design, advertising and branding, she's been inspired by Photography, Digital Art and Tech Innovations. She loves smart creative packaging design.

www.pinterest.com/masciari

Marina Goñi

Marina Goñi is a little studio located in Getxo (Spain) dedicated basically to creation and management of brands. Their work consist of finding that thing that makes each enterprise special and reinforces it, making it visible and recognizable.

www.marinagoni.com

Marty Weiss and Friends

Marty Weiss and Friends is a design and branding company in New York City founded on the belief that no matter how much business may change, the value of great ideas never does.

They have specialized in brand make-overs and brand launches for many of their clients, including A/X Armani Exchange, Grand Central Terminal, Waterworks and Sobieski Vodka to name a few. Their aim is to create unique visual, verbal and behavioral language that is both visceral and powerful to anyone exposed to a brand – from employees to shareholders; to the trade and consumers. Key capabilities include strategic and creative consultation, logo and brand identity, advertising, digital and web design, packaging, point of sale, collateral, etc.

www.martyweissandfriends.com

Maryana Sharenkova & Kristina Savinskaya

Maryana Sharenkova had graduated from University of Print Arts in Saint-Petersburg; Kristina Savinskaya was studying in Moscow State University of Arts and Industry.

cargocollective.com/yanasharenkova

Mathias Martin

Mathias Martin works for public areas such as hotels and restaurants.

mathias-martin.es

Memo / Douglas Riccardi

Douglas Riccardi established himself early-on as a leading-edge visual designer with an innate capacity for strategic thinking. He worked with some of the most influential and innovative international design firms of their time, including Tibor Kalman's M&Co (New York), Benetton SpA (Treviso, Italy) and Ettore Sottsass's Sottsass Associati (Milan, Italy).

Returning to the US in 1993 to form his own firm, Riccardi envisioned MEMO as a category-defying studio: its creative and strategic talents would touch every aspect of brand identity via the language of design. As lead designer and strategist, Riccardi is involved with every studio account, whether conceiving a brand's identity or ensuring it evolves with relevance and power.

MEMO values every client relationship as symbiotic – holding the belief that each party can learn from the other. It is another reason why they feel so strongly invested in a client's success and often become a trusted strategic partner. MEMO can boast that most clients have been partnering with them for eight years or more..

www.memo-ny.com

O

Oscar Bastidas Villegas

Oscar Bastidas Villegas (AKA Mor8) is a 32-year-old Venezuelan Art Director, with more than 10 years of experience working for international brands like Toyota, Buchanan's, McDonalds, Jhonnie Walker, Budget among others, with main beacon on branding and advertising projects.

Also he has been involved in illustrations and designs for other clients like Snop Clothing (Venezuelan clothing line), Pollen (United Kindom Electronic Music Label) and participated in exhibits like "In Vino Veritas" from the graphic collective "La Casa Tomada".

www.mor8graphic.com

P

Para Todo Hay Fans ®

Para Todo Hay Fans ®(Eng) is an online marketing agency based in Guadalajara, Jalisco, Mexico, founded by Federico V. Astorga in 2010. They provide solutions for the creation, diffusion and promotion of clients' brands through the internet. Their services include: Web development, Multimedia Services, Branding, Online Marketing, Social Media and Advertising. Their work is recognized and applied worldwide. They have worked with countries such as Italy, Canada, USA, Czech Republic, Russia, Australia, England, Egypt, Greece, Switzerland, Argentina and Colombia.

www.paratodohayfans.com

Peck & Co.

p.112-113
Peck & Co. is a creative shop in Nashville, TN with a focus on brand identity, logo design and packaging design.

www.peckandco.com

Phil Robson

p.188-189
Phil Robson is a UK based award winning graphic designer, artist and director. Since winning the new designers award in 2003 Phil has worked with motion graphics studios, post houses, advertising agencies and brands around the world. Phil's style is bold and graphic, a trait he uses in both his design and art executions. Phil's design direction work has gained recognition internationally with Promax, being awarded two gold awards and finalist at Australia's Award, for best on-air branding and best ident design. Further exposure throughout international design publications such as Creative Review, Computers Arts UK, Creative AUS, CG China, Territory Indonesia and the Laurence King 3d Type book, as well as hits on Fubiz and Motionographer. Whilst as ARTIST FILFURY, Hypebeast, Complex, Sneaker Freaker and High Snobiety have all featured his work.

www.cortezstreet.com

Planet Creative

p.156-157, 208-209, 218-219, 224-225
Planet Creative was founded in 2004 and is located in Stockholm, Sweden. It is a branding agency focusing on corporate culture and visual identities. Their work covers the entire brand building chain. From idea to execution.

www.planetcreative.com

Polygraphe

p.190-191
Polygraphe is a Montreal based graphic design and brand identity studio.

polygraphe.ca

PUNK YOU BRANDS

p.080-081
PUNK YOU BRANDS is a Siberia-based Russian branding agency, founded in 2009. It specializes in brand development, communication strategies and creative concepts. It is founder of International Festival of Advertising and Design Concepts FAKESTIVAL. It's entered the Top 10 best Russian branding agencies since 2011, according to AKAR (www.akarussia.ru).

www.punk-you.ru

R

Rene Herman

p.144-145
Rene Herman is a tireless lover of typography and a collector of wisdom. She revels in conceptual thinking and design that makes a difference and causes human flourishing. She also has a healthy appetite for copious amounts of tea.

www.behance.net/reneherman

Revert Design

p.130-131
Revert Design is a graphic design studio, founded in 2013 by Trevor Finnegan.

The focus of the company is to create functional and beautiful design for a growing number of clients over a range of different areas. Revert Design offers complete professional design, web, and photography services, with an emphasis on brand development. They believe that good design is good business.

www.revertdesign.net

RoAndCo

p.132-133
RoAndCo, founded in 2006 and led by award-winning Creative Director Roanne Adams, is a multi-disciplinary creative agency that serves as a visual thought leader for a range of forward-thinking fashion and lifestyle clients. As branding experts, Roanne and her team work quickly and intuitively to pinpoint the most essential, visceral quality with which to tell a company's story and visually captivate its audience. As creatives—whose services include graphic design and art direction for print, web and video—they're known for bringing clients a cool cachet and a contemporary look while remaining grounded in a love of the classics, from old movie typography to modernist art to the work of mid-century design icons. With a diverse roster of talents hailing from Brazil to Japan, the agency aims to thoughtfully distill a client's inspiration, ideas and motivations into fresh, sincere and compelling brand messages that engage and resonate.

roandcostudio.com

Rod Castro

p.194-195
Rod Castro, creative designer and director, graduated from Universidad de Monterrey and Art Center College of Design, specialized in brand development and creative solutions.

www.rod-castro.com

S

SabotagePKG

p.228-229
SabotagePKG is a multidisciplinary design agency based in London EC2. The agency specialises in branding, packaging & trends for the FMCG and luxury brands sectors.

sabotagepkg.com

Scandinavian Design Group

p.136-139
Scandinavian Design Group, the Scandinavia's leading design and innovation agency with more than 25 years of experience. They work with a number of Scandinavian and international brands covering identity development, packaging and retail design, digital and interactive design, and innovation and growth. Their clients represent some of Scandinavia's largest companies such as Statoil and EVRY - but also start-ups and niche brands like Hovelsrud, KORK, and Rom & Tonik. They love using their passion and experience on any design challenge, and find inspiration in working with both large organizations and small entrepreneurs. They believe that design drives growth, and that design begins with people. So understanding needs, desires and preferences is always their starting point. From the creation of brands, products and services to changing perceptions or inspiring a company, their solutions have a compelling simplicity—revealing potential, initiating possibilities and realising ambitions.

www.sdg.no

Scott Naauao

p.200-201
Scott Naauao is a Senior Designer, Art Director, Animator and Photographer with 7 years' working experience in building brands, creating ad campaigns, designing websites and print collateral, and producing motion graphics for commercials and films.

naauao.com

Sean Gallagher

p.146-149
Sean Gallagher is a designer/artist who specializes in hospitality design.

Whilst living in London he created and ran a company called "Set" which was aimed towards offering a complete design/marketing package for hospitality business owners.

He now resides and works on a multitude of design and art based jobs in Sydney, Australia.

www.seangallagher.com.au

SeeMeDesign

p.088-089
SeeMeDesign is a small design shop located in Atlanta, GA, USA specializing in brand strategy development. They are known for their creative concepts and approaches to both new and old ideas, working with small to mid-size businesses, corporations, non-profits, cities and communities. Their mission is to help businesses thrive, one passionate business owner at a time. Their process is genuine. They care. They get to know the business, team and environment, consider the psychology behind their purpose and market, and then they build.

www.seemedesign.com

Sherman Chia J.W

p.100-101
Sherman Chia J.W is a graphic designer that has always loved challenging the brief and redefining the traditional. His focus lies mainly in packaging and branding. His work methodology is that he does prefer an open mind when approaching each brief and to explore as widely and as wildly as possible, there after will he rope himself back in and go through his ideas. For him as a creative, he stands that "if you don't go all out to discover the moon, how do you know that its possible."

Sherman draw his inspiration from everything and anything such as architecture, typography, music, food blogs and even just window shopping. He does feel that we find the best ideas in the most unlikely of places.

shermanjw.com

Smart! Grupo Creativo

p.184-185
Smart! Grupo Creativo is a multidisciplinary team of professionals in graphic design, communication and information technology.

Under the values of commitment, interpretation, advice, and prompt action, they provide communication strategies for corporate identity, adding value and ensuring the brand reach its full development.

They work in all stages of brand development process such as visual identity design, editorial design, packaging, website design, corporate communication and art direction.

www.smartgc.com.ar

Somewhere Else

p.056-059
Somewhere Else is about the constant shift away from the ordinary; the persistent journey to create work that goes beyond the basal need to communicate.

They are the dreamers, the outsiders and the shamans that conjure new stories and mythologies. Through their approach and processes, they provide distilled solutions for businesses.

Together with their broad range of selected clients, they push to create unique works that are idea-driven, relevant and intelligently crafted.

www.somewhere-else.info

Squad Ink

p.210-211
Squad Ink is a full service, Sydney based, strategic branding and design agency led by creative directors and brothers, Matthew and Terry Squadrito. With a focus on brand identity, their craft is intuitively driven, expansive and robust and unfolds across digital, print, experiential and packaging mediums.

www.squadink.com

Stir and Enjoy

p.060-061, 216-217
Stir and Enjoy helps food and beverage industry clients identify areas of opportunity and solve ongoing business challenges through beautiful brand design and engaging brand experiences. From naming to overall concept and expression to ongoing management, promotion and development, Stir and Enjoy ensures consistently strong personality at every consumer touch point and irresistible brands built to last.

www.stirandenjoy.com

Studio Hausherr

p.186
Studio Hausherr is a small graphic design agency based in Berlin. Their work focuses on corporate, editorial and web design for clients in the field of art, fashion and culture. They provide a comprehensive design and visual communication tailored to suit clients' needs.

www.studiohausherr.com

Studio WABA

p.202-203
Studio WABA is an independent graphic design studio based in Porto, Portugal, specializing in brand communication, corporate identity, editorial design, exhibition design, and packaging. Its goal is to create honest, intelligent, and timeless work. It takes care of every single step of the graphic design process and collaborates with its clients, big or small, to create thoughtful responses that reflect their needs and values. The team also co-works regularly with architects, interior designers, photographers, web developers, interaction designers, and copywriters to accomplish a full-pack solution for their projects.

studiowaba.com

T
The Birthdays™

p.099
The Birthdays™ is the collaboration of Konstantina Yiannakopoulou & George Strouzas sharing time between real life and design. They believe in design as science, in form through composition, in type as form, in symbols, in communication through concept, through justification and through clarity. Effective communication, specificity and uniqueness always remain the goal.

www.behance.net/TheBirthdays

The Plant

p.118-119, 212-215
The Plant was born in 2003 in East London, and still lives there. It's a boutique design agency, packed with gifted designers, strategists, writers and project managers from all over the world. They are all experts in brand creation, who love turning a challenge into something beautiful.

The Plant has worked with many exciting clients, including Jamie Oliver, Masterchef, Eat, Frae frozen yoghurt, London fashion weekend and art 14.

www.theplant.co.uk

W
WonderEight

p.036-037, 078, 223
WonderEight is a Beirut based design agency, working for international and local companies who like to challenge their customers and want to be different and daring. Benefiting from their cultural diversity, they innovate in the fields of branding and visual communication. Their strategic location in the gate of the Middle East allows the team to bridge between western and eastern brands and to create concepts that work in their environment while introducing new ways of co-creation.

Founded in 1999 by Nasrala brothers Boudy and Walid, today, with Karim Abourizk also on board it gathers a handful of highly skilled creative designers, web developers and marketing strategists who enjoy a bespoke work environment, made to inspire and interact with the local design and art community. This creative space regroups a design agency, a prototyping workshop, a facility fortrainings and talks, a handpicked book library and an art exhibition space.

This multifaceted environment keeps on renewing itself and creates a constant synergy between their clients, the public and themselves.

www.wondereight.com

Wan Ling Su

p.163
Having engaged in graphic design for 3 years, Wan Ling Su specializes in the application of hand-painted elements, and is also good at the use of geometric elements and the coordination of colors.

www.behance.net/13smile

ACKNOWLEDGEMENTS

We would like to express our gratitude to all of the designers and companies for their generous contribution of images, ideas, and concepts. We are also very grateful to many other people whose names do not appear in the credits but who made specific contributions and provided support. Without them, the successful completion of this book would not be possible. Special thanks to all of the contributors for sharing their innovation and creativity with all of our readers around the world. Our editorial team includes editors Daniela Huang / Shirley Lam, to whom we are truly grateful.